W9-ARG-323

ST. JOSEPH'S UNIVERSITY   STX
PN1047.T913 1981
The problem of verse language /

PN1047.T913 1981

Yuri Tynianov

The Problem of Verse Language

PN
1047
.T913
1981

Edited and translated
by

MICHAEL SOSA & BRENT HARVEY

Ardis / Ann Arbor

236331

Tynianov
The Problem of Verse Language

English translation

Copyright © 1981 by Ardis

No part of this publication may be reproduced
without the written permission of the publisher,
Ardis, 2901 Heatherway, Ann Arbor, Michigan 48104

Library of Congress Cataloging in Publication Data

Tynianov, IUrii Nikolaevich, 1894-1943.
 The problem of verse language.

  Translation of Problema stikhotvornogo iazyka.
  1. Poetics. 2. Russian poetry—History and criticism.
I. Title.
PN1047. T913 1981   801'.951   81-1158
ISBN 0-88233-464-6   AACR2

TABLE OF CONTENTS

INTRODUCTION TO *THE PROBLEM OF VERSE LANGUAGE*

The exact date of Tynianov's entry into Opoiaz [*Obshchestvo izu-cheniia poeticheskogo iazyka* — Society for the Study of Poetic Language] is not known, although his development toward the Formalist method is well-documented. In his autobiography,[1] Tynianov tells us he was born in 1894 into the family of a doctor, in Vitebsk province. He entered the University of St. Petersburg in 1912, registering in the department of Slavic and Russian studies. It was here, in the seminar on Pushkin conducted by Professor S. A. Vengerov, that Tynianov quickly assimilated, and began to go far beyond, the traditional biographical approach of his professors. (Boris Eikhenbaum and Boris Tomashevsky also took part in this seminar.) In his autobiography, Tynianov lovingly recalls the figure of the aging Vengerov, who succumbed to the enthusiasm and iconoclastic spirit of his students, and allowed his seminar to become a laboratory for the developing Formalists. Tynianov describes how Vengerov would often reminisce about his personal meeting with Turgenev himself, and yet would take part in the discussions of the seminar with the cheerful abandonment of a neophyte. Although he did not enter Opoiaz until 1919 or 1920, the general direction and content of Tynianov's method was established while still in the university. As he writes in his autobiography: "I began to study Griboedov . . . I read a lecture on Kiukhel'beker. Vengerov brightened up. He began to clap. Thus my work began."

Despite the fact that Tynianov's first published work was concerned with two prose writers *(Dostoevsky and Gogol: Toward a Theory of Parody)*, and that a good deal of his time was absorbed in the writing of historical novels, we can safely say that it was verse and the problems of verse language which lay at the heart of Tynianov's work. In his autobiography, and in many of the memoirs concerning Tynianov,[2] we learn that his first and deepest commitment was to poetry and to the particular problems posed by the structure of verse.

The work which we know as *The Problem of Verse Language (Problema stikhotvornogo iazyka)* was published in 1924 in Leningrad by the Academia Press. It was part of a series entitled "Questions of Poetics" ("Voprosy poetiki"), which included Tomashevsky's *Russian Versification* and Boris Eikhenbaum's *Through Literature*. The original title of the work, however, was not *The Problem of Verse Language*, but *The Problem of Verse Semantics (Problema stikhovoi semantiki)*. Tynianov had been working in and around problems of semantics in verse for several years. In 1919 he read a series of lectures entitled "Language and the Image" at the House of Arts. He revised and expanded his material during the next few years, delivering two lectures to the State Institute of the History of Arts in Leningrad entitled "The Problem of Verse Semantics." These lectures were read on February 25 and March 4, 1923. Tynianov also read his work to gatherings of Opoiaz at this time. The work was completed and ready to print, but for some unknown reason, it was decided to first publish the above-mentioned texts of Tomashevsky and Eikhenbaum. In a letter to the critic Lev Lunts, written in January 1924, Tynianov informs him that the publisher became frightened of the title *(The Problem of Verse Semantics)*. The publisher changed it, therefore, to *The Problem of Verse Language.* Tynianov had already prepared a preface to the work, believing it would be published under the title he wished. Upon learning of the title change, however, he wrote a new preface, roughly the same length as the initial one. The two prefaces generally are concerned with the same project, that is, the elucidation of the tasks which the author had set himself. In the first, unpublished version, however, Tynianov does spend another paragraph or so examining the problems and contradictions of Potebnia's theory of the image. What is important here is not any earth-shaking revelation of Tynianov's "original plans" in the unpublished variant, but simply the fact that Tynianov himself felt a different type of introduction was necessary upon learning of the title change. For this reason we have included the first foreword, entitled "Preface to *The Problem of Verse Semantics.*" (This preface appears in his collection *Poetika, istoriia literatury, kino* [M. 1977].) The second preface, which Tynianov wrote and published after learning of the new title, is found in its proper place, immediately preceding the first chapter of the text.

The reader may safely work his or her way through this complex and at times quite difficult text by keeping in mind the fact that there is a thread which runs through each and every investigation presented. This link is present both in Tynianov's analyses of actual poems and in every theoretical pronouncement made in the text, no matter how far removed some of these pronouncements may seem from the realm of "poetry." In the preface Tynianov writes:

> The recently advanced concept of "poetic language" is undergoing at present a crisis, undoubtedly brought about by the breadth and diffusiveness of the volume and content of this concept at the psycho-linguistic level. The term "poetry" which we have in language and in science has currently lost its specific volume and content and has an evaluative coloring.
>
> The concrete concept of *verse* (in contradistinction to the concept of *prose)* and the features of *verse* (or rather *versified)* language is the subject of my analysis in this book.

In this brief excerpt from the preface, we see that Tynianov is actually concerned with two projects in the text. The first, but not necessarily the most crucial, is the separation of the concept of "poetry" from that of verse. To Tynianov, "poetry" is a pre-scientific conglomeration of undistilled emotions and hazy, subjective opinion. The author very seldom uses the term "poeziia" ("poetry"), and when he does, it is usually placed in quotation marks or used in an ironic way. As he states clearly, it is *verse* ("stikh") which is the subject of analysis here. All the material conditions which we associate with verse structure are placed in the foreground by Tynianov. It is these conditions, or features, of verse only which may be subjected to thorough scientific investigation. Verse, then, is a noetic object rather than an emotional one. (As we will see, Tynianov does not deny the existence of emotionality on a certain level of verse. He stresses, however, that this emotionality is a secondary property, and is always defined and limited by the particularities of the verse structure itself.)

Having separated verse ("stikh") from poetry ("poeziia"), Tynianov goes on to use the term "stikh" in a much more crucial way. It is precisely in this second examination of verse, which now stands in opposition to *prose*, that the theoretical pivot of the text is located. The central question which subordinates all others in the text to itself is this: what are the specific conditions of verse? In other words, when we decide to assign a particular work of verbal art to either the order of prose or the order of verse, which elements of that work prove to be the decisive ones? To use the language which Tynianov and Jakobson would use in their celebrated joint theses ("Problems of the Study of Language and Literature," 1928), what specifically separates verse from all other areas of intellectual activity? As Professor Jakobson points out via the pun in his paper "Yury Tynianov in Prague" (see Appendix I), the defining of the specificity of one's area of inquiry was the dominant concern of the majority of Russian Formalist texts. In order to be worthy of the title of "science," literary theory and criticism must pass beyond description of subjective states of mind. It must define and delimit in concrete ways the distinguishing features of a particular subset of verbal activity.

The Problem of Verse Language, then, quite naturally falls into two complementary chapters. In the first of these, which is entitled "Rhythm as the Constructive Factor of Verse," Tynianov theorizes on the above-mentioned features of verse. By working through various problems of previous theories in this area, he arrives at a set of structural laws which he sees operating in all verse constructs. These he calls his "laws of verse." In Chapter Two, entitled "The Sense of the Word in Verse," Tynianov applies these "laws" and examines the various ways in which they reveal themselves in selected European verse.

Before Tynianov can begin the search for the distinguishing factors of verse construction, he is forced to define the very term "construction." As we will see, this is a necessary prelude, for the author is battling an incredible number of misconceptions and simplifications concerning terms used in any type of analysis of verbal art. As Tynianov will say many times, such concepts

11

as "form," "composition," and "content" have been taken out of the realm of dynamic phenomena. The following excerpt from the first section, entitled "The Concept of Construction," describes the foundations upon which Tynianov will construct his theory:

> We have only recently overcome the celebrated analogy: form-content = glass-wine. But all spatial analogies applied to the concept of form are important in that they only pretend to be analogies. In actual fact, a certain static element, intimately connected with spatiality, invariably slips into the concept of form. (Instead of this, one should recognize even spatial forms as dynamic *sui generis.*) This is also true of terminology. I would be so bold as to maintain that the word "composition," in nine out of ten cases, covers up this attitude toward form as a static phenomenon. Imperceptibly, the concept of the "line" or the "stanza" is taken out of the realm of the dynamic . . . . There appears the dangerous concept of "symmetry of compositional facts," dangerous because there can be no talk of symmetry where one finds amplification.
>
> The unity of the work is not a closed, symmetrical intactness, but an unfolding, dynamic integrity. Between its elements is not the static sign of equality and addition, but the dynamic sign of correlation and integration.
>
> The form of the literary work must be recognized as a dynamic phenomenon.
>
> This dynamism reveals itself firstly in the concept of the constructive principle. Not all factors of a word are equivalent. Dynamic form is not generated by means of combination or merger (the often-used concept of "correspondence"), but by means of interaction, and, consequently, the pushing forward of one group of factors at the expense of another. In doing so, the advanced factor deforms the subordinate ones. The sensation of form is always the sensation of the flow (and, consequently, of the alteration) of correlation between the subordinating, constructive factor and the subordinated factors . . . . Art lives by means of this interaction and struggle . . . . If this sensation of the *interaction* of factors disappears . . . the fact of art is obliterated. It becomes automatized.

This lengthy quotation was necessary to convince the reader of the vast distance which Tynianov has placed between himself and previous theoreticians of verse. Rather than viewing "form" as a spatial equivalent of "content," Tynianov examines every feature of the work of art as formal, in the quite literal sense of the word. These features are not fitted together, like glove and hand, nor do they "correspond" to each other in some metaphorical way. (Here we see Tynianov engaging in polemics with some of the most basic concepts of Symbolist verse theory. Coming of age in the first two decades of the twentieth century, he would have been immersed in Symbolist versification, philosophy, and vocabulary. This topic, however, must remain undeveloped here.) Each work of verbal art, whether it be verse or prose, is a struggle of contending factors. It is this struggle, this disparity between the various components of the work which causes it to be recognized as a work of art.

An extremely important ramification of Tynianov's conception of form must be dealt with. The various elements which go to make up the work do not simply interact with each other, creating art by means of this open-ended interaction. Rather, each work of verbal art presents a hierarchy of functions. Only one of these functions at any one time can be the dominant one. This dominant element, of course, may shift in the course of the work. That feature of the work which dominates and subordinates all other features to itself Tynianov calls the constructive factor. This conception of the hierarchy, then, illuminates the path which the investigation into the specific features of verse must follow. In order to arrive at a solution to the problem of verse, one must decide which element of the verse construct subordinates all others to itself. In other words, what is the constructive factor of verse?

Tynianov first eliminates what the constructive factor of verse is not. Already in the preface, he has neatly done away with those theories which hold that the peculiarities of verse are located in its language. Here Tynianov associates these theories with the nineteenth-century philologist Alexander Potebnia, who was a professor at Kharkov University for many years. Potebnia's basic conception was that poetry uses language in an aesthetically-organized fashion, while prose language is practically-oriented. For Potebnia, the study of verse meant the study of poetic language, and the utilization of metaphor and image-making which that language rested upon.[3]

In the preface Tynianov writes:

A. A. Potebnia determined for quite a considerable time ways of handling this question with the theory of the image. The crisis of this theory was called forth by the lack of delineation and specification of this image. If an everyday colloquial expression and an entire chapter of *Eugene Onegin* are both presented as an image, then the question arises: what is the specificity of the latter? And this question moves aside and replaces the questions which are advanced by the theory of the image.

A second approach which Tynianov deflates in the course of Chapter One is that of the school of *Ohrenphilologie*. From this viewpoint, verse is characterized as an acoustic phenomenon, one which is intimately connected with recitation and the declamatory arts. Although recognizing the fact that the acoustic feature had advanced to the foreground in verse in the opening decades of the twentieth century, Tynianov reminds the reader that it remains

13

a secondary feature, and cannot in and of itself define verse as a system. In order to display the contradictions inherent in *Ohrenphilologie*, Tynianov presents several poems of Pushkin, in which the poet uses dots, rather than words, as essential features of the text. These dots, which have been characterized as "omissions," or "unwritten fragments," are, in fact, features of the verse construct, even though we find it impossible to present them acoustically:

Mir opustel . . . .
. . . .
. . . .
. . . .

The world has grown empty . . . . .
. . . .
. . . .
. . . .

In relationship to poems such as these, Tynianov introduces the concept which he calls the *"equivalent of the text."* An equivalent of the text is any substitution of non-verbal elements in place of verbal ones. In Pushkin's poems we see that the graphic feature plays quite an important role. (This concept of the equivalent is not only useful in displaying the limitations of *Ohrenphilologie*, however. As we will see later on, Tynianov is quite flexible with this dynamic conception. In analyzing *vers libre* as a system taking part in the verse series, Tynianov will utilize the concept of the *equivalent of meter*. Literary texts in the prose order, he reminds us, are also filled with equivalents. In Gogol's short story "The Nose," we see various grotesque *equivalents of the hero.*)

Tynianov's own theory concerning the constructive factor of verse still faces two formidable challengers, which may be dealt with together. They are the system of *vers libre* and rhythmical prose. Following the radical experimentation with verse as a system in the late nineteenth century, particularly in France, many theoreticians and poets had spoken of the final destruction of the boundary between the two. Tynianov himself confesses that *vers libre* is the typical verse construct of the twentieth century. The poem in prose, supposedly, revealed that what had previously been conceived of as two distinct realms were in fact not. Simultaneously, approaching this problem from the "other end of the scale," theoreticians of prose began to realize that a good deal of prose writing was just as rich in sound texture, just as "metrically arranged" and even just as "rhythmical" as verse. Tynianov mentions the experiments which Guyau performed on metrical articulations in the works of Rabelais and Zola. Grammont compared verse of Francis Viele-Griffin and Gustave Kahn with passages from novels of Flaubert. In

14

Russia, the prose works of the Symbolist poets were phenomena of the same type. Bely's *Petersburg* and *Kotik Letaev* and Sologub's *The Petty Demon* come to mind immediately. *Vers libre* and rhythmical prose were placed together here, for they actually are dealing with the same problem in relationship to defining the specific features of verse. They both, in fact, deny the existence of any qualitative leap between the verse order and the prose order. Verse and prose are viewed as part of the same continuum, which might be called the "aesthetic" use of language. Since the graphic arrangement on the page no longer gives a hint as to which realm the text belongs, this must mean that this particular concern of ours is outdated.

Tynianov's solution to the above problem, concerning those features of verse which separate it from the realm of prose, in turn refutes all of the theoretical challenges which he faces in Chapter One. The theoretical stance which holds that there is no longer any distinguishing feature of verse is just as incorrect as the conception of verse as an acoustic system. Potebnia's investigations into the features of poetic language also will be countered here. The basic fault with all of the above is that they retain a static conception of form, as well as a static conception of the constructive factor, i.e., that factor which subordinates all others to itself. The problem with those theoreticians who view the prose poem or the novel written in rhythmial prose as basically the same type of phenomenon is that they view rhythm as something which is simply added to language in order to achieve something called "form." The constructive factor, argues Tynianov, keeping in mind the hierarchical conceptions presented earlier, necessarily deforms and limits all secondary factors of the work. The verse series is defined and separated from the prose series by the fact that, within its boundaries, rhythm is no longer secondary. That is, rhythm in verse is a type of "imperialist power," as Tynianov jokes in the text. It forces all other elements of the poem to work for its own ends. The mistake of Potebnia was that he analyzed a secondary feature of verse incorrectly as the constructive factor. The approach of *Ohrenphilologie*, likewise, did not recognize the ways in which rhythm distorts and leads acoustic phenomena in its own direction. And finally, rhythmical prose and *vers libre* are, in fact, distinct species. Borrowing heavily from the linguistic terminology used by his colleagues, Tynianov argues that the qualitative leap between the two lies in the functional significance of rhythm. In the prose series, the constructive factor is semantics, which will subordinate all other features, including rhythm. Rhythm in prose, therefore, is a secondary component, dependent upon meaning. The exact opposite is true in verse. Here, semantics becomes a subordinated factor, one which is severely deformed by the structural peculiarities of rhythm. In Section 7 of Chapter One, entitled "The Function of Rhythm in Verse and in Prose," Tynianov writes:

> No matter how much phonic, in the broad sense of the word, organization accompanies prose, it does not result in prose becoming

15

verse. On the other hand, however nearly verse approaches prose in this regard, it will never become prose.

This is precisely the *raison d'etre* that "rhythmical prose" exists within the prosaic series, and *vers libre* exists within the verse series. (If we were to set a good part of our *vers libre* into prose, hardly anyone would be able to read it.) The "poem in prose" as a genre, and the "novel in verse" as a genre are based on the disparity between their respective phenomena, and not on their proximity. The "poem in prose" always reveals the essence of prose, while the "novel in verse" reveals the essence of verse . . . . Thus, the distinction between verse and prose as being systematic and unsystematic in the phonic relationship to speech is refuted by the facts themselves. The distinction is located in the area of the functional role of rhythm. It is precisely this functional role of rhythm which is decisive.

Having defined rhythm as the constructive factor of verse, Tynianov in turn must define rhythm itself. In Section 5 of Chapter One, "Meter and Rhythm," he theoretically separates the two phenomena. We find the definition of rhythm quite broad and extremely flexible. To Tynianov, rhythm is simply the "dynamic grouping of material." Meter, however, is the "dynamic grouping of vocal material according to an accentual indication." At the same time, Tynianov theorizes that meter is a necessary component of rhythm. He is completely aware, of course, of the presence of *vers libre* when making this statement. The way in which he deals with this seeming contradiction is quite fascinating. As was stated previously, Tynianov's conception of the equivalent is quite a flexible one. Here he presents the theory that *vers libre* utilizes various equivalents of meter in order to restore dynamism to verse. Equivalents of meter, argues Tynianov, come forth during those epochs when traditional meter, with its quite regular accentual patterns, has become effaced and automatic. *Vers libre*, then, with its "lack" of accentual indication, renews the dynamism of verse material:

> Thus, meter as a regular accentual system may be absent. The basis of meter lies not so much in the presence of a system, as in the presence of its principle. The principle of meter consists of the dynamic grouping of vocal material according to an accentual indication. The most simple and basic phenomenon here will be the isolation of some metrical group as a unit. This isolation is simultaneously a dynamic preparation for the following, similar (not identical, but similar) group. If this metrical preparation is allowed, we have before us a metrical system . . .
>
> But what if the dynamic preparation is not allowed in the following similar group? In such a case, meter ceases to exist in the shape of a regular system, but it does exist in another way. "Prohibited preparation" is also a feature which creates dynamism . . . . Such verse will

16

metrically be free verse, *vers libre, vers irregulier.*

Advancing in a logical fashion, Tynianov moves from his definition of rhythm to attempting to define those features of the verse construct which promote rhythm. These he calls the "laws of verse." With these four brief theoretical statements, Tynianov closes Chapter one. The practical ramifications of these "laws" will be taken up in Chapter Two, but it is necessary to list them here, since they are an extremely important part of the theoretical equipment which the author carries into the second half of his work:

Thus, the factors of rhythm are:
1. the factor of the unity of the verse series;
2. the factor of its compactness;
3. the factor of vocal material being made dynamic, and
4. the factor of the successiveness of vocal material in verse.

In Chapter Two, "The Sense of the Word in Verse," we see Tynianov introduce and apply the body of theory developed previously to various verse constructions. Besides this, he presents detailed examinations of various prose constructions, examining diverse aspects of their structure in an attempt to discover basic laws operating in semantics. Tynianov's project here is to reveal the dynamics of everyday, prosaic speech which the reader of verse brings to the text. He examines, then, the distortion and deformation of these general laws of semantics by the "laws of verse," and by the subordinating feature of rhythm in verse. Briefly, then: rhythm is the constructive factor of verse, dominating and turning all laws of prosaic semantics in a particular direction, that direction which is functionally advanced in the particular poem.

Tynianov's semantic analyses are not complex, but it is important to have a firm grasp on the terminology which he develops in Chapter Two. First he examines the inherent dualism of all "definitions" of words—that is, words do not have only one meaning. There is the basic conception which most people will associate with a particular word, and there are also alterations of this basic meaning depending upon context and function. In English, we might differentiate between "meaning"and "sense." Hermann Paul contrasted the "usual" meaning to the "occasional" meaning, while Benno Erdmann utilized the terms "Sachvorstellung" and "Bedeutungsvorstellung." What Tynianov wishes to emphasize here is that the meaning of a word cannot exist in isolation. That is, an isolated word, what Tynianov calls the "dictionary" word, does not exist in a pristine state, totally free of all interfering context. It only exists, he argues, in other particular conditions, in those conditions which we have come to place particular isolated words, for no matter what reasons. We see then, that Tynianov is attuned to the inevitable deforming role of context in every particular case. We also see that his

17

approach borrows heavily from the groundwork of functional linguistics being laid at the time in Moscow.

Tynianov deals with the question of semantic dualism by demonstrating various usages of the same word. In presenting four distinct conceptions of the word "earth" ("tellus," "humus," "Boden," "Land"), he probes the semantic category which allows these usages to nevertheless be considered as united in some way. This phenomenon he calls the category of lexical unity. Those semantic features which are retained in each distinct usage of the word Tynianov calls the *principal sign* ("osnovnoi priznak") of meaning. The semantic overtones and nuances which advance in the word in particular environmental situations are relegated to the realm of *secondary signs* ("vtorostepennye priznaki") of meaning. Developing this concept of secondary signs, Tynianov presents nine distinct usages of the word "man" ("chelovek"), and also carefully analyzes the syntactic structures which promote the advancement of particular secondary signs. For example, in some cases, the word is deformed or colored by its environment and receives a *group coloring,* in Tynianov's terminology. In others, it is found in an isolated position: "In high rank let him not forget / The holiest of callings: man" (Zhukovsky).

Another important term which Tynianov introduces here is the *oscillating sign* of meaning. The oscillating sign may be of two types. The first type advances when two principal signs are potentially present in a given word, and we see them crowd each other. The most obvious example of this is the pun. Each principal sign will remain unstable in the pun precisely because of the presence of the other. Tynianov also points out that there is a second type of oscillating sign. Here the principal sign of a particular word is displaced by the function which the word bears in a particular usage. An example of this displacement is the usage of swear words in an endearing way. The intonation used overrides the principal sign of the swear word, while the swear words carry what Tynianov labels *lexical coloring:*

> These words carry the function of filling in the emphatic intonation with vocal material. Here the principal sign of meaning of the words is effaced, and the *lexical coloring* remains as a connecting link, placing a given word in a particular series. The sense and strength of such a usage of a word, with a lexical coloring which opposes its intonational coloring, lies precisely in the sensation of this lack of convergence . . . . A lexical element which is opposed to the emotional and intonational coloring compels it to advance all the more strongly.

Having explained these basic semantic rules, and having developed a working terminology for them, Tynianov devotes the remainder of Chapter Two to examining the action of these rules in verse. Here we will observe how principal and secondary signs of meaning, as well as oscillating signs and lexical coloring, are assimilated and distorted by conditions of verse structure.

Tynianov will examine how rhythm, as the constructive factor of verse, and his "laws of verse," which promote rhythmical grouping, subordinate the operational rules of semantics.

"The Influence of Verse on the Sense of Words"(Sec. 3, Chap. Two) is the theoretical and practical pivot of the second half of the work. Here Tynianov analyzes the ways in which rhythmical grouping alters both the meaning and the sense of words introduced into verse. The first "law of verse," *the factor of the unity of the series,* is explained in the following way:

> The rhythmical verse series presents an entire system of conditions which distinctively influence the principal and secondary signs of meaning and the appearance of oscillating signs.
>
> The first such factor is the *factor of the unity of the series.*
>
> Every verse series isolates and intensifies its own boundaries. More weakly isolated, but nevertheless isolated, are the internal divisions of the series—the boundaries of periods, etc.

Here we see that verse is a construction based on division. Each segment which is obtained as a result of this division Tynianov calls a series. The series may be of varying size. One type of basic series will be the line. If the line is fragmented by a comma, then we will have the half-line constituting a series. Speaking in broader terms, the stanza is also another type of series. (Particular problems associated with translating the word "riad" as "series" will be discussed in the closing section of this Introduction.) What is important here is that the series, as such, is isolated by the verse construct. This isolation promotes the unity of that particular series, no matter what the particular semantic content of that series might be. This unity, Tynianov asserts, will be a much tighter one than could ever be achieved in a prosaic statement. Intimately connected to the first "law of verse" is the second: the factor of the compactness ("tesnota") of the verse series. Because of this fact of syntactic isolation of the series, each word within that series will enter into a much more intimate (and deforming) relationship with every other word. As an example of the above laws, Tynianov quotes one of Tyutchev's poems:

> *Kak bednyi nishchii, mimo sadu*
> *Bredet po zharkoi mostovoi.*

> Like a poor beggar, past the garden
> He wanders along the hot roadway.

The unity and compactness of the series in this case was responsible for a misreading of the two terms of comparison. Despite the comma in the middle of the first line, which signifies "someone wandering past the garden like a poor beggar," many readers understood the following signification: "like a

19

poor beggar past the garden—he wanders."

Tynianov's third and fourth laws of verse are extensions of the first two. They also rest on the basic feature of division, brought about by rhythmical grouping. As was noted above, the syntactic isolation of the series promotes its unity and compactness. As a result of this, the semantic feature of every word introduced into the verse structure is greatly enhanced. This process of the sharpening of the semantic element of the word Tynianov calls the "dynamization" ("dinamizatsii") of vocal material. Although the term is quite clumsy in English, it is not so in Russian. The process of "dynamization," Tynianov argues, promotes the enlivening of the principal sign in the word. Verse structure advances the principal sign so strongly that we are forced to recognize its presence.[4]

The final "law" of Tynianov, which he calls the factor of the successiveness of vocal material in verse, remains to be described. In verse, words in a given series, because of the compact unity promoted by isolation, will be much more dependent upon one another. They will also deform each other in certain ways not possible in a prose construction. The word is only introduced into verse under very tight restrictions. That is, it must fill in a rhythmical gap in a given series, buts its interaction with the other words will cause certain secondary or oscillating signs of meaning to appear, which must be taken into account. Vocal material introduced into verse becomes part of a particular succession. Tynianov contrasts the conception of the *successiveness* of vocal material in verse with the *simultaneity* of vocal material in prose. That is, the constructive factor of prose is semantics. In order to achieve an understanding of a particular clause, it must be taken in as a unity. The prose construction must not allow individual words to enter into intimate and deforming relationships with each other, for the final meaning of the construction as a whole would then be upset.

Let us sum up with Tynianov's words from the closing section ("The Question of the Image") of his study:

> Therefore, dynamic form unwinds in the complex interaction of the constructive factor with that which is subordinated to it. The constructive factor deforms that which is subordinated to it. This is why it is useless to return to the investigation of the abstraction of the "word," existing in the consciousness of the poet and connected associatively with other words. Even these associative connections proceed not from the "word," but are directed *by the general dynamics of the structure.*

NOTES TO THE TRANSLATOR'S INTRODUCTION

1. Iu. Tynianov, "Avtobiografiia," *Sochineniia* (Moscow-Leningrad, 1959), vol. 1.

2. *Iurii Tynianov: pisatel' i uchenyi* (Moscow, 1966).

3. Although a good deal of Formalist ink was spilled in the attempt to counter the basic positions of Potebnia, we must recognize the fact that his approach to verse was in no way original. In the nineteenth century, when historical linguists and philologists all over Europe were attempting to analyze the diverse forms of language as such, this basic division between verse and prose was nearly always made along the same lines. "Potebniaism," then, is not simply a Russian phenomenon.

4. A much more radical and sweeping conception of this process is seen in Viktor Shklovsky's "Resurrection of the Word." In this paper Shklovsky argues that the advancement of this effaced principal sign is, in fact, the function of art.

ACKNOWLEDGEMENTS

Thanks are due to Professor J. Thomas Shaw of the University of Wisconsin-Madison for supporting this project, and for his most thorough reading of the text. Without his invaluable suggestions and store of practical knowledge as a translator, this text would be a good deal more mediocre. The translator is also grateful to Professor James Bailey of the same university for his careful reading of the translation, and for his suggested ways of dealing with certain ambiguities. I would also like to thank Professor Lawrence Thomas for his translations of Shevchenko's Ukrainian, and the Serbian of Koshutich. Last, but certainly not least, the translator is extremely grateful to Professor Roman Jakobson for the use of his paper, "Iurii Tynianov v Prage."

Michael Sosa
University of Wisconsin-Madison

A NOTE ON THE TRANSLATION

Tynianov's language, like that of most of the Russian Formalists, is at times quite difficult to penetrate. This is not due to pedantry on his part, but rather to the density of his thought and to his ability to use every resource of the Russian language. The problem for the translator is not a failure to understand what point Tynianov is attempting to establish, but rather how this point may be said again in comprehensible English. One of Tynianov's favorite devices is to coin totally new Russian verbs, in which he is aided by the " -ovat' " ending. For example, we have heard the term "semasiology," but how does one translate "semasiologovat' "?

Tynianov also makes use of subtle distinctions in his noun endings, which are weakened in translation. The best example is the following: "dinamika ("dynamics") vs. "dinamizatsiia" ("the process of making dynamic"). The distinction to be made is that between a state of being and an ongoing process. For this reason one Russian term is often conveyed by several English words. There are places in the text where Tynianov himself used quotation marks. Here the translators felt free to coin a proper English term, and also to place it in quotation marks. Where Tynianov's terminology is especially tricky, we have placed the Russian word in parentheses after our English equivalent.

Several of the choices of the translators need to be explained in further detail. Perhaps the most frequently encountered, and most flexible, of Tynianov's terms is "series" ("riad"). It must be emphasized that the author uses the term in two quite distinct ways. First, in separating the realm of prose from that of verse, Tynianov refers to the "prose series" and the "verse series." Another possible translation would be "order" or "realm." We see this same usage of "riad" when Tynianov speaks of the "historical series" and the "literary series." The second usage of the term "riad" is applied only to those segments of verse material which result from the process of rhythmical grouping in verse. As was mentioned earlier, this "series" may vary in size, ranging from the half-line to the line, or even to the stanza or the poem as a whole. The most common "series" which Tynianov speaks of is the unit of the line.

The terms which were translated as "principal sign" ("osnovnoi priznak") of meaning and secondary signs ("vtorostepennye priznaki") of meaning should be mentioned. Translating "priznak" as "sign" does present problems. There are two words in Russian for two distinct concepts. "Znak" literally means "sign," in the sense of a "symbol." "Priznak" has a more limited meaning—an "outward indication." One can see, however, that to conceptualize an "outward indication of meaning" would be a difficult task in itself. Therefore, "sign" was chosen for both Russian terms.

The remaining problems are small, and can be mentioned together. The Russian word "ustanovka" can be quite complicated. It literally means "arrangement." It can also mean "directions," "lines," or "goal," "aim." Tynianov most often uses the term in the sense of "aiming toward" something: "ustanovka na dialekt" ("aiming toward a dialect"). Often the English word "orientation" may be used for this. However, there are times when Tynianov uses the words "orientatsiia"and "ustanovka" in the same sentence, and is obviously making some distinction between the two. Therefore "ustanovka" is not always translated as "orientation." For the term "razvertyvanie," "unwinding" was used almost exclusively. However, once or twice "unfolding"appeared to be less clumsy.When Tynianov distinguishes between the material part ("veshchestvennaia chast' ") of the word and the formal part ("formal'naia chast' "), he is basically contrasting the root with formatives and affixes. The term which was translated as "sound repetition" should also be discussed. Here Tynianov is using a specialized term developed by Osip Brik, "povtor," and not the Russian word for "repetition" ("povtorenie"). Brik was analyzing the phenomenon of sound repetition specifically, and for that reason we have narrowed down the translation of the term as well.

In translating the poems, we in no way were attempting to create works of art in the English language. Tynianov's analyses very often depend on the word order in the Russian poem. Therefore, we were compelled to retain this identical word order in English, or to retain as much as possible. Because of this, a good deal of some of the greatest Russian verse sounds quite crude in our versions. The "poems" in English are, in fact, plain prose translations which retain the verse structure. The crucial problem here was to make Tynianov's analyses of various verse constructions clear, even to the non-Russian reader. It was Tynianov's view, and it is our view, that the "laws of verse" which he works out in the text do not apply only to Russian verse. Precisely because Tynianov does not place the center of gravity of the verse construct in the areas of versification or metrics, the laws worked out here are equally applicable to nearly all verse which comes under the umbrella of the European tradition.

One of the major tasks which the Formalists placed before themselves was the establishment of a tight and rigorous scientific vocabulary. Tynianov is no exception to this rule. As the study develops, he uses a certain precise set of terms again and again. To refuse to recognize this fact by coming up with catchy synonyms would be to destroy the value of the text as a scientific inquiry into the structure of verse. This translation has not been simplified, nor abridged, nor Americanized in any way. It has also not been made to appear more complex than it actually is. As one will soon discover, Tynianov's "laws of verse" are actually quite few in number.

M.S. & B. H.

Yuri Tynianov

PREFACE TO *THE PROBLEM OF VERSE SEMANTICS*

The study of verse has made great strides recently. It should develop in the near future into an entire field, although its parameters were staked out comparatively recently.

Until recently, however, the study of poetic semantics (that science concerned with the meanings of words and of verbal groups, and their development and alteration in poetry) has been pushed to the side.

The last significant phenomenon in this area was the theory of the image, presented for the most part by Potebnia. The defects of this theory are now more or less obvious. If an ordinary, everyday colloquial expression and an entire chapter of *Eugene Onegin* are both presented as an *image*, then the question arises: what is the specificity of the *poetic* image?

For Potebnia, this question did not exist. This occurred because he transferred the center of gravity beyond the parameters of the particular *construction*. Every image and every poetic work are joined together at one point—the point of the *idea*, which lies beyond the parameters of the image or the work. This point—X—opened the door to a great number of metaphysical speculations. As a matter of fact, the *dynamism* of poetry was swept away quite on the sly. If the image leads to X, what is important is not the flow of the image (or the image itself), but this synchronous (simultaneous) X. This X lies outside the image; consquently, as many images as one chooses may join in this X.

The price which Potebnia's departure from construction pays is the blending of phenomena of various constructions—of colloquial speech and of verse—into a homogeneous mass. Being blended, they do not explain each other, but rather crowd and obscure each other.

Potebnia-ism perished in this contradiction. After him, the study of the sense of the poetic word proceeded quite haltingly. This same defect— the ignoring of the constructive, *structural* feature in language—is taken in quite another direction by one person even now: the study of the sense of the poetic word from the point of view of the individual linguistic consciousness of the poet.[1] It is obviously only possible to trace psychological associations and the coupling of verbal groups by any given poet, and to pass this off as the study of poetic semantics, by substituting the poet for poetry. One must assume that there exists in a particular poet some firm and unilateral individual linguistic consciousness, not dependent upon the construction in which it is set in motion. But linguistic consciousness varies, in dependence upon the *structure* in which it is set in motion. The coupling of images by one and the same poet will be identical in identical genres, but will be

25

different in different genres. It will follow one path in prose, and another in verse.

The present work attempts to investigate the specific features of the sense of words, in dependence upon verse construction.

Therefore, to the abstraction of the "word," I counterpose the concrete "word in verse." I repudiate the diffuse concept of "poetry," which as a term has managed to acquire an evaluative coloring, and has lost its real volume and content. Instead, I examine one of the most fundamental constructive categories of verbal art—verse.

In the first chapter I elucidate the constructive factor of verse, that which forms (or, more exactly, deforms) all others.

The second chapter is concerned with the essence of the question, which is precisely those specific alterations of the sense of the word which occur under the influence of the constructive factor of verse.

My work was completed in the winter of 1923. Since that time several books and articles have appeared bearing some relation to its subject matter. They have been only partially utilized.

Parts of the present work were read to Opoiaz[2] and to the Society for Artistic Literature in the Russian Institute of the History of Arts. To those members who took part in the discussion, I express my gratitude.

I am especially obliged to S. I. Bernshtein[3] for his valuable advice and help.

I dedicate my work to the Society with which it is intimately connected—Opoiaz.[4]

---

1. Tynianov refers to V. V. Vinogradov, and his work on the poetry of Anna Akhmatova.

2. Acronym for "Obshchevstvo izucheniia poeticheskogo iazyka" ("Society for the Study of Poetic Language"). The society was formed in St. Petersburg in 1916-17, taking shape around the *Collections on the Theory of Poetic Language (Sborniki po teorii poeticheskogo iazyka).* Its members included Viktor Shklovsky, S. I. Bernshtein, Boris Eikhenbaum, Lev Yakubinsky, E. D. Polivanov, B. A. Larin, V. A. Piast, M. A. Slonimsky, and others. Tynianov did not enter Opoiaz until 1919 or 1920.

3. Sergei Ignat'evich Bernshtein (1892-1970), Russian linguist and theoretician of verse language.

4. This preface first appeared in the collection of Tynianov's works entitled *Poetika, istoriia literatury, kino* (M. 1977).

THE PROBLEM OF VERSE LANGUAGE

PREFACE

The study of *verse* has recently made great progress. Although we will recall the systematic beginning of this study, it undoubtedly should develop in the near future into a complete field.

On one side of the study of verse stands the question of poetic language and style. Studies in this area have been detached from the study of verse, leaving the impression that this poetic language and style are not bound together with verse and do not depend upon it.

The recently advanced concept of "poetic language" is undergoing a crisis at present, undoubtedly brought about by the breadth and diffusiveness of the volume and content of this concept at the psycho-linguistic level. The term "poetry" which we have in language and in science has currently lost its specific volume and content, and has an evaluative coloring.

The concrete concept of *verse* (in contradistinction to the concept of *prose*) and the features of *verse* (or rather *versified*) language is the subject of my analysis in this book.

These features are defined on the basis of the analysis of verse as a construction in which all elements are found in reciprocal correlation. Therefore, I will attempt to supply in connection what is generally analyzed in an isolated manner, namely, the study of the elements of style.

The most significant question in the study of poetic style is the question of *the meaning and sense of the poetic word.* For quite a considerable time Potebnia determined the ways in which the question of the theory of the image was handled. The crisis of this theory was called forth by the lack of delineation and specification of this image. If an everyday colloquial expression and an entire chapter of *Eugene Onegin* are both presented as an image, then the question arises: what is the specificity of the latter? And this question moves aside and replaces the questions which are advanced by the theory of the image.

The aim of the present work is precisely the analysis of the *specific* alterations of *the meaning and sense of the word* dependent upon the very *verse* construction.

This demanded from the author a substantiation of the concept of verse as a construction. This substantiation he gives in the first part of the work.

Parts of the present work were read in the winter of 1923 at the Society for the Study of the Theory of Poetic Language (Opoiaz) and the Society for the Study of Artistic Literature, part of the Russian Institute for the History of the Arts. I wish to express my gratitude to the members who took part in the discussions there. I offer special thanks to S. I. Bernshtein for the valuable things he pointed out. While this work was being written, several books and articles have appeared which bear some relation to this subject. They could be taken into account only partially.

Razliv, 5/VII 1923

CHAPTER ONE

RHYTHM AS THE CONSTRUCTIVE FACTOR OF VERSE

1. The Concept of "Construction"

The study of verbal art is beset by two difficulties. The first is that of the material being given shape, the most simple conventional designation of which is speech, or the word. The second is that of the constructive principle of this art.

In the first case, the object of our investigation proves to be something quite intimately connected with our everyday consciousness, and sometimes even depends upon the intimacy of this connection. We willingly overlook the specifics of this connection, and arbitrarily introducing to the object of study all the attitudes which have become habitual in our daily existence, we make them the starting-point of our investigation of literature.[1] Along with this, we overlook the heterogeneity and multiple significance of the material, which depends upon its role and purpose. We overlook the fact that in the word there are unequal features, depending on the word's functions. One feature may be emphasized at the expense of the rest, resulting in the deformation of the remainder, and in their sometimes being brought down to the level of neutral props. The grandiose attempt of Potebnia to construct a theory of literature, inferring from the word as $\check{\epsilon}\nu$ ["the one"] the complex artistic creation as $\pi\tilde{\alpha}\nu$ ["the many"], was doomed in advance to failure, for the essence of the relationship of $\pi\tilde{\alpha}$ to $\pi\tilde{\alpha}\nu$ is in the heterogeneity and diverse functional significance of this "$\pi\tilde{\alpha}\nu$". The concept of "material" does not exceed the boundaries of form, for it is also formal; the confusion of this concept with extra-constructive features is erroneous.

The second difficulty is the habitual attitude toward the nature of the constructive forming principle as being *static*. We will make this clear with an example. It was not so long ago that we left behind that type of criticism which discusses (and censures) the heroes of a novel as if they were living people. Neither can anyone guarantee that biographies of heroes will finally disappear, or the attempts to restore historical reality according to these biographies. These are all based on the prerequisite of a *static hero*. Here it is appropriate to recall the words of Goethe on artistic fiction, concerning the double light on the landscapes of Rubens and the contradictory facts in Shakespeare:

> In a situation in which a picture becomes a genuine painting, the artist is granted freedom, and he is able to resort to *fiction*. The artist speaks with the aid of the *whole*. This is why the light from two sides, even

31

though it does violence to, and is against nature, is still higher than nature.

Lady Macbeth, who at one time says: "I nursed my children with my breast," and about whom it is then stated: "she has not children" is justified, for Shakespeare was "concerned about the strength of each given speech":

> In general one should not understand in a too narrow or petty sense the word of a poet or the stroke of a painter. The poet compels his characters *in a given place* to say precisely what is demanded, what best produces a precise impression, and is not particularly concerned, nor is he considering that it might be in obvious contradiction with something that was said in another place.

Goethe also explains this from the point of view of the constructive principle of Shakespearian *drama:*

> In general Shakespeare scarcely would have thought, as he wrote, that his plays would be printed, that his lines would be counted, compared, and collated. It is more likely that before his eyes was a stage. He saw how his plays moved and lived, how quickly they passed before the eyes and flew past the ears of the audience. He saw that one cannot stop to criticize details, but must be concerned only about how to create the strongest impression in the present moment.[2]

And so, the static unity of the hero (as, in general, every static unity in a literary work) proves to be quite unstable. It is completely dependent upon the principle of construction and may fluctuate in the course of the work, so that each separate case is determined by the general dynamics of the work. It is sufficient that there is a sign of unity—its category—which legitimizes the most abrupt cases of its actual violation, compelling us to look upon them as *equivalents of unity.*[3]

But such a unity, it is quite obvious, is not the naively-conceived static unity of the hero. Instead of a sign of static intactness, there is the sign of dynamic integration and integrity. There is no static hero, only a dynamic hero. The sign of the hero or the name of the hero is sufficient so that we do not examine attentively in each given case the hero himself.[4]

In this example of the hero, the strength and stability of static habits of consciousness are revealed. This is also exactly how matters stand concerning the question of the "form" of a literary work. We have just recently overcome the celebrated analogy: form - content = glass - wine. But all spatial analogies applied to the concept of form are important in that they only pretend to be analogies. In actual fact, a certain static element, intimately connected with spatiality, invariably slips into the concept of form. (Instead

32

of this, one should recognize even spatial forms as dynamic *sui generis.*) This is also true of terminology. I would be so bold as to maintain that the word "composition," in nine out of ten cases, covers up this attitude toward form as a static phenomenon. Imperceptibly, the concept of the "line" or the "stanza" is taken out of the realm of the dynamic. Repetition ceases to be recognized as a fact of varying strength in various conditions of frequency and quantity. There appears the dangerous concept of "symmetry of compositional facts," dangerous because there can be no talk of symmetry where one finds amplification.

The unity of the work is not a closed, symmetrical intactness, but an unfolding, dynamic integrity. Between its elements is not the static sign of equality and addition, but the dynamic sign of correlation and integration.

The form of the literary work must be recognized as a dynamic phenomenon.

This dynamism reveals itself firstly in the concept of the constructive principle. Not all factors of a word are equivalent. Dynamic form is not generated by means of combination or merger (the often-used concept of "correspondence"), but by means of interaction, and, consequently, the pushing forward of one group of factors at the expense of another. In so doing, the advanced factor deforms the subordinate ones. The sensation of form is always the sensation of the flow (and, consequently of the alteration) of correlation between the subordinating, constructive factor and the subordinated factors. It is not obligatory to introduce a *temporal* nuance into this concept of flow, or "unfolding." Flow and dynamics may be taken as such, outside of time, as pure movement. Art lives by means of this interaction and struggle. Without this sensation of subordination and deformation of all factors by the one factor playing the constructive role, there is no fact of art. ("The *co-ordination* of factors is a type of negative characterization of the constructive principle."   V. Shklovsky.) If this sensation of the *interaction* of factors disappears (which assumes the compulsory presence of *two* features: the subordinating and the subordinated), the fact of art is obliterated. It becomes automatized.

In this way a historical nuance is introduced into the concept of the "constructive principle" and the "material." But the history of literature also convinces us of the stability of *fundamental principles of the construction and of material.* The system of metrico-tonic verse of Lomonosov, formerly a constructive factor, joined around the time of Kostrov with a fixed system of syntax and vocabulary. Its subordinating, deforming role was weakened and verse became automatic, which demanded the revolution of Derzhavin in order to break the merger, and to return again to interaction, struggle, and form. The most important feature here proves to be that of a new interaction, and not simply the introduction of some factor in and of itself. Introducing, for example, an effaced meter (which has been effaced precisely because of a strong, habitual merger of meter with the accentual system of the clause and

33

with certain lexical elements), bringing it into interaction with new factors, we renovate meter itself and refresh the new constructive possibilities in it. (Such is the historical role of poetic *parody.)* The introduction of new meters results in the renewal of the constructive principle in meter.

The fundamental categories of poetic form remain steadfast. Historical development does not shuffle the cards, nor does it destroy the distinctions between the constructive principle and the material. On the contrary, it emphasizes this distinction. This does not eliminate, in and of itself, the problems of each given instance, with its own individual correlation of the constructive principle and the material, with its own problem in individual dynamic form.

I will introduce one example of the automatization of a certain system of verse, and the rescue of the constructive significance of meter by means of the breakup of this sytem. It is interesting that the agent of this breakup is that same *ottava rima* which A. Maikov sees as a model of the "harmony of verse."[5] In the 1830s iambic tetrameter had become automatized. Consider Pushkin's *Little House in Kolomna* : "I am bored by iambic tetrameter" ("Chetyrekhstopnyi iamb mne nadoel").

In 1831 Shevyrev printed a dissertation in *The Telescope* entitled "On the Possibility of Introducing the Italian *Ottava Rima* into Russian Versification," with a translation of the seventh canto of *Jerusalem Delivered.* The fragment was published for 1835 in the *Moscow Observer* with the following foreword:

> This experiment . . . had . . . the misfortune to appear in an epoch of *harmonious* monotony, which was then heard in the world of our poetry and which filled our ears, beginning to bore us a little. These *ottava rimas,* where they *violated all the habitual rules of our prosody,* where they announced a complete divorce from masculine and feminine rhyme, *where the trochee was mixed in with the iamb, where two vowels were taken as one syllable,*—these octaves, frightening with all the sharpness of their innovations, were made possible at exactly the same time that our hearing *cherished a type of sweet bliss of monotonous sounds, when thought slumbered peacefully beneath the melody and the tongue reduced words to nothing but sounds.*[6]

Here we see perfectly characterized the automatism which is a result of habitual blending of meter with the word. It is necessary to do violence to "all of the rules" in order to restore the dynamics of verse. The *ottava rimas* provoked a literary storm. I. I. Dmitriev wrote to Prince Vyazemsky:

> Professor Shevyrev and ex-student Belinsky have long ago buried not only our own fraternity of old men, but, and do not be angry, yourself, Batyushkov, and even Pushkin. The professor declared that our *stiff*

(this is a stylish word) meter and our *stiff* language of poetry are unsuitable and *monotonous* (also a favorite word). By way of a model he published in the *Observer* a translation in *ottava rima* of the seventh canto of *Jerusalem Delivered*. I would like it if you would compare it with Raich's translation, and tell me if you find in the meters and poetic language of Shevyrev the musicality, the strength, and the expressiveness which, according to him, are missing in the Russian poetry of our time. . . It is difficult, however, to outlive our fathers' language and to begin anew with our ABC's.[7]

Everything in this argument is typical: the attitude of the old poet to "musicality" and generally to verse as a congealed *system*, the statement that the revolution of Shevyrev is a return to the ABC's (to elementary fundamentals), and the attempt of Shevyrev to renew the dynamic interaction of factors of verse at the expense of effaced "musicality."

Shevyrev himself published a provocative epigram on his *ottava rimas:*

> *Rifmach, stikhom rossiiskim nedovol'nyi,*
> *Zatial v nem likhoi perevorot.*
> *Stal stikh lomat' on v derzosti kramol'noi,*
> *Vsem rifmam dal beschinneishii razvod.*
> *Iamb i khorei pustil guliat' po vol'noi*
> *I vsekh grekhov kakoi zhe vyshel plod?*
> *Dozhd' s voplem, vetrom, gromom soglasilsia*
> *I strashnyi mir garmonii oglushilsia.*[8]

The rhymester, displeased with Russian verse,
Ventured upon an intrepid overturn.
He began to break up verse with seditious impudence,
To all rhymes he gave outrageous divorce.
Iambs and trochees he let walk about freely,
And what was the fruit of all these sins?
A downpour of shouts with the wind and thunder agreed
And the terrible peace of harmony was deafened.

Pushkin in turn called the automatized verse a "canape" ("sofa"), but equated dynamic and new verse with a *jolting* cart bouncing along a bumpy road. "New verse" was not good because it was "more musical" or "more perfect," but because it renewed the dynamics in the relationship of factors. Such is the dialectical development of form, modifying the correlation between the constructive principle and that which is subordinated to it. Thus the constructive role of this constructive principle is preserved.

2. The Unmotivated in Art as the Material of Study

The preceding comments force us to give an account of the material of literary study. This question is not one of indifference for the investigator. The choice of material inevitably entails as its consequence some direction for the investigation, and this in part predetermines the very conclusions, or else limits their meaning. Clearly, our object of study, which claims to be the study of *art*, must be made specific, thereby distinguishing it from other areas of intellectual activity. We take these as either its material or its instrument. Every work of art presents a complex interaction of many factors. Consequently, coupled with the problem of the investigation is the problem of the definition of the specific nature of this interaction. In facing the restriction of the material and the impossibility of the application of experimental methods of study, it is easy to take secondary properties of these factors, resulting from their status *in a given case*, as their *fundamental* properties. Therefore, general erroneous conclusions are being applied to instances in which the given factors evidently play a subordinating role.

From this point of view, the outwardly easy and simple area of *motivated art* turns out to be quite complex and unfavorable material for study. Motivation in art is the justification of some single factor from the point of view of all others, i.e., its co-ordination with the others (V. Shklovsky, B. Eikhenbaum). Each factor is motivated by its connection with everything else.[9]

The deformation of factors brought about by this is carried out evenly. The inner motivation, which occurs on the constructive level of the work, smooths over, as it were, their *specifica*, making art "light" and acceptable. Motivated art is deceptive. Karamzin suggested that "old words be given a new sense, offered in a new form, but so skillfully as to deceive the reader and conceal from him the unusualness of the expression."[10]

But precisely for this reason, the study of the functions of any one factor is even more difficult to conduct on light art. The investigation of these functions does not mean the investigation of what is quantitatively typical, but rather what is qualitatively characteristic of the general elements in relation to other fields of intellectual activity. This is to find the specific "plus" of art. Therefore, in motivated works of art, what is characteristic is the very motivation (the concealment of this "plus"), which is a distinctive negative characteristic (V. Shklovsky), rather than a positive one. This is to say that the concealed functions of factors may not serve as criteria for the overall study of literature.

This is proved correct in the course of literary history. The motivated, "exact" and "light" art of the Karamzinians was a dialectical rebuff of Lomonosov's principles, the cultivation of the self-sufficient word in the "senseless, resounding" ode. A literary storm was initiated, as the smoothness and motivation was clearly recognized as a negative sign.[11] Thus arose the concept of "difficult lightness." Batiushkov, counterposing the "light" verse of *poesie fugitive* to the outwardly "difficult" verse of the ode, maintained that "light verses are the most difficult." (Consider his *later* words: "Who now does not write light verse?")

In order to evaluate the equilibrium of factors, it is necessary to know the functions which balance each of the factors with the others. Therefore, it would be most fruitful in such a study to investigate those instances where a given factor is advanced (is unmotivated).

Here those phenomena are treated which are combinations or conjugations of the factors of one (internally motivated) series with the factors of another, alien (but also internally motivated) series, creating the phenomenon of a hybrid series. The most simple example of such a combination is poetic *parody*, where, for example, the meter and syntax of one (fixed) series is brought into interaction with the vocabulary and semantics of another. If one of these series is familiar to us, having been given earlier in some work, then the study of such a parody involves analysis of a type of experiment, where some conditions are altered while others remain the same. In separating out these conditions, and observing the altered factors, conclusions may be drawn concerning the connection and dependence of one factor on another (its combinatory functions). The course of the history of poetry, apparently, justifies such a choice. Revolutions in poetry, upon close examination, usually prove to be phenomena involving the conjugation or combination of one series with another. (Consider V. Shklovsky's indication that turning to "younger branches" is in part a turn toward the comic.) For example, the so-called "trimeter," in common usage in the service of comic verse in French poetry of the 17th century, is united by the Romantics with vocabulary, semantics, etc. of the elevated style, and becomes "heroic verse" (Grammont). A more recent example: Nekrasov fused the habitual meter of the high lyric (the balladic) with the lexical and semantic (in the broad sense) elements of another series.[12] In our own time, Mayakovsky has fused the form of comic verse with a system of grandiose images. (Compare his verse with that of P. Potemkin and others of the *Satirikon.)*

Thus, in order not to run the risk of making erroneous theoretical conclusions, we must work on material with a perceptible form. The task of literary history is, by the way, the baring of form. With this point in view, literary history, the elucidation of the character of the literary work and its factors, is a kind of dynamic archeology.

The investigation of a factor in and of itself, and not with the aim of the elucidation of its functions, may be carried out on a wide range of material where the constructive property is not elucidated. However, even here there are limits, which in the end prove to be the tacitly implied limits of a series with one broad constructive sign. Thus the investigation of meter, as such, cannot be carried out with equal validity on verse material and on the material of newspaper articles.

The elucidation of the constructive function of some factor is most conveniently undertaken on literary material of an advanced or displaced series (unmotivated). Motivated instances, as instances bearing a negative character, are less convenient for this, just as the function of the formal elements of a *word* are more difficult to observe in cases where the word has a negative formal character.[13]

One further preliminary remark. The constructive principle may be connected by habitual associations with the typical system of its application. However, the concept of the constructive principle does not coincide with the concept of the systems in which it is applied. Before us is the infinite variety of literary phenomena, a plurality of systems of interacting factors. However, in these systems are generalizing lines and divisions, embracing a great quantity of phenomena.

That factor or condition which is observed in the most extreme phenomena of one series, without which the phenomenon crosses over to another series, is the necessary and sufficient condition for the constructive principle of the given series.

And if we fail to consider these *extreme instances on the periphery of the series*, we might easily identify the constructive principle with the system of its application.

Not everything in this system is equally necessary nor equally sufficient for some phenomenon to be related to some particular series of construction. *The constructive principle is recognized not in the maximum of conditions which create it, but rather in the minimum of conditions.* Obviously, these minimal conditions are more closely connected with a given construction. Therefore, it is in these conditions that we must look for answers concerning the specific character of the construction.

The importance of the constructive feature, and of the concept that it does not coincide with the system in which it is applied is proven by the fact that this system may be excessive. The most simple example of this is the *accidental rhyme.*

Zhukovsky, starting from a legitimate 18th-century device, rhymes in his early verses: "nebes"–"serdets" ("heaven"–"heart"), "pogibnet"–"vozniknet" ("perish"–"arise"), "gorit"–"chtit' ", ("burn"–"to honor") ["Dobrodetel' "–"Virtue", 1798], "syny"–"l'vy" ("sons"–"lions"), "velikoserdnyi"–"prevoznesennyi" ("great-hearted"–"exalted") ["Mir"–"Peace", 1800]; "nepravosudnoi"–"nepristupnoi" ("unjust"–"unapproachable"), "voznest' "–"perst' " ("raise"–"finger"), "mechem"–"sonm" ("sword"–"assembly") ["K cheloveku"–"To the People", 1802]. And these rhymes are quite acceptable, although "inexact." (In the given case, they are also acoustically acceptable.) However, we refuse to consider the following as rhymes: "sostavliet"– "osveshchaet" ("put together"–"illuminate") ["Blagodenstvie Rossii"–"Prosperity for Russia", 1797]; "sooruzheny"–"oblozheny" ("built"–"taxed") ["Dobrodetel' "–"Virtue", 1798]; "rek"–"breg" ("river"—"shore") ["Mogushchestvo, slava i blagodenstvie Rossii"—"Power, Glory and Prosperity for Russia", 1799]. These irreproachable rhymes are encountered in *unrhymed verses*. The rhyme, therefore, is an extraconstructive fact. As a fact of rhythm, that is, of construction, such "accidental rhyme" is uncommonly remote *sui generis* in its constructive tasks and consequences from ordinary rhyme.

3. The Role of Ohrenphilologie *in the Orientation of the Constructive Factor of Verse*

The period of literary revolutions experienced by us for the past several decades has raised the question of the constructive principle of poetry with exceptional force. This may be because the paths of literary revolutions cut across unmotivated and mixed forms. The rise of the acoustic feature in verse has played the decisive role in this period. The so-called school of *Ohrenphilologie,* asserting that verse exists only as sound, sprang up in regular connection with the general movement of poetry. In the movement of poetry there apparently exist definite shifts of such periods: periods when the acoustic feature is emphasized in verse, which are replaced by periods when the acoustic character of verse seemingly weakens and other aspects of verse are emphasized at its expense. Likewise, different periods are characterized by accompanying phenomena in the area of literary life of such things as the exceptional development of recitation (in Germany and in Russia during the past decade), an intimate connection of declamatory art with poetry (the declamation of poets), and so on.[14] (These phenomena have already begun to fade, and will probably fade away completely.)

This period (both in poetry and in the scholarship on poetry) has helped to reveal a fact of extreme importance. It has posed the problem of the constructive significance of *rhythm.*

In the 1890s Wundt wrote:

In ancient verse the rhythmical form influences verbal content to a very high degree, but in contemporary verse, the latter is enveloped in a rhythmical form which acquires a freer and freer movement, occasionally even adapting itself to being used for effect. The distinction of this form from ordinary speech is not in its being subordinate to certain metrical laws, but rather that the rhythm achieved by the arrangement of words corresponds exactly to the emotional coloring of the words and thoughts.[15]

And yet Potebnia wrote that "the delimitation of activity in general does not lead to its depreciation":

In Indo-European languages, several musical properties of words (such as the distinction of ascending and descending stresses, drawing-out, bringing simple speech nearer to recitative, raisings and lowerings, amplification and weakening of the voice as means of differentiating separate words) tend to disappear. At the same time, there grows up from one side the euphony of connected speech and verse, and the development of song, of vocal music, from another... Thus vestiges of former stages of development, while separating, are not effaced, but are deepened.[16]

Thus while Wundt allots a quite modest role in modern poetry to rhythm (by which he understands accentual regularity), Potebnia shows that this growing differentiation simultaneously promotes the lowering of musical (that is, of rhythmical elements in the broad sense of the term) elements of conversational speech, and the amplification of the same elements in poetry. (This indication, however, is not related to the general system of Potebnia.) The approach to verse as sound has helped to elucidate this deepening difference and has led to extremely important results, which lie, however, outside the tasks and possibilities of *Ohrenphilologie*.

Meumann has distinguished two opposing tendencies in the recitation of verse, according to the method (and perhaps the object) of classification[17]:

There are two tendencies of poetic recitation, which now struggle with each other, now unite and agree. At times each takes upon itself the task of creating a rhythmical impression. I shall call them the measuring tendency *(taktierende Tendenz)* and the phrasing (grouping) tendency *(gruppierende, phrasierende Tendenz)*. In the first there is properly manifested a *rhythmical* necessity *(Bedürfniss)*, an arrangement in terms of a rhythmical ordering of our consecutively flowing experiences, in terms of the evenness of temporal intervals between major rhythmical features. In the second an independent interest in *content* is advanced. But such a disposition of the movement of presentation does not allow a thorough schematization of its own flow. Meaningful recitation compels us to continually lower the rhythmical principle.[18]

This tendency to single out unified rhythmical groups revealed the specific essence of verse, expressed in the subordination of the unifying principle of one type to the unifying principle of another. Here verse is revealed as a system of *complex interaction, and not of combination.* Metaphorically speaking, verse is revealed as a struggle of factors, rather than as a collaboration of factors. It becomes clear that the specific plus of poetry lies precisely in the area of this interaction, the foundation of which is the

40

constructive significance of rhythm and its deforming role relative to factors of another order. (The original comic element of the measuring tendency resulted precisely from the sharp sensation of this *deformation*.) The complexity of the problem of verse in the broad sense is revealed in its unmotivated quality.

But even the second, contrary tendency of recitation plays its role (although a negative one) in revealing that something in verse, and in determining the specific construction of verse. Neatly meaningful phrasing, not coinciding with the rhythm, unintentionally raised the question of the functions of rhythm. Here rhythm proves to be superfluous, binding, an interfering principle. Poetry proves to be deteriorated prose, and the *raison d'etre* of verse becomes questionable. With meaningful phrasing, enjambment, for example, ceased to exist not only as a rhythmical device, but as a device in general. The tendency to set off only meaningful groups lowered the very concept of enjambment, which is the *failure to converge* rhythmical groups with syntatico-semantic ones. Since the unifying principle proved to be syntactico-semantic (the striving toward unification in grammatical units), then of what type of failure to converge can one speak?

It is natural that defenders of this tendency must come to the defense of *vers libre* as more "free" than a rhythmical construction (Meumann).

All of this overlooked that specificity must be related to factors of another order—to the special, selected poetic vocabulary, to devices habitual to poetry, to syntactic classification, etc. Here, of course, the borders between verse and poetic prose are effaced. *The elimination of rhythm as a major, subordinating factor leads to a lowering of the specificity of verse, thus emphasizing once again its constructive role in verse.*

At the same time, the acoustic approach to verse created the possibility of expanding the concept of rhythm, which originally had been restricted to the narrow area of the accentual system. The concept of rhythm became unusually complex and diverse, undoubtedly as a result of the approach to verse from the observation point of acoustics, which created the possibility of an unusually subtle observation of phenomena. In this respect, Professor Saran is correct when he says that "the puny metrics of the previous epoch, with its paper determination, it resting on an exceptionally schematic foundation, and its scanning approach, lost the right to existence since the work of Sievers."[19]

Thus, the acoustic approach to verse revealed the antinomy of poetic creation, which had previously seemed steady and flat.

But, concealing within itself internal contradictions, the acoustic approach to verse is not able to handle the solution of the problem which it itself has raised.

41

4. The Acoustic Approach to Verse and its Inadequacy

On one hand, the acoustic approach does not exhaust the elements of artistic creation, and on the other, it even creates superfluous ones.

The understanding of verse as sound collides most of all with several essential facts of poetry which are not exhausted by the acoustic display of verse, and even stand in contradiction to it.

Above all of these stands the fact of the *equivalents of a text*. I call the equivalent of a poetic text anything which *substitutes* extra-verbal features for the text, above all its partial omissions, such as a partial substitution with graphic features, etc.

Let us introduce several examples.

In Pushkin's poem "To the Sea" ("K moriu"), the thirteenth stanza usually reads in the following way:

> *Mir opustel... Teper' kuda zhe*
> *Menia b ty vynes, okean?*
> *Sud'ba liudei povsiudu ta zhe:*
> *Gde kaplia blaga, tam na strazhe*
> *Il' prosveshchen'e, il' tiran.*
> *Proshchai zhe more...*

> The world has grown empty... Now where
> Would you take me, ocean?
> The fate of people is everywhere the same:
> Where there is a drop of blessing, there stand guard
> Either enlightenment, or a tyrant.
> Farewell then, sea...

However, this stanza, already totally finished, was subjected to a curious alteration. In the 1824 text only two words were retained:

> *Mir opustel. . . . .*
> . . . .
> . . . .
> . . . .
> The world has grown empty. . . .
> . . . .
> . . . .
> . . . .

After this came three and one-half lines of dots with the comment:

42

"In this place the author has placed three and one-half lines of dots. This poem was delivered to the publisher by Prince P. A. Vyazemsky in its original state, and is printed here just as it came from the pen of Pushkin himself." In the 1826 edition, instead of the three lines:

> Sud'ba liudei povsiudu ta zhe:
> Gde kaplia blaga, tam na strazhe
> Il'prosveshchen'e, il'tiran—

> The fate of people is everywhere the same:
> Where there is a drop of blessing, there stand guard
> Either enlightenment, or a tyrant—

there are placed two lines of dots; but in the 1829 text, the last in his lifetime, Pushkin again retained only the first phrase:

> Mir opustel...

> The world has grown empty...

Again there followed three and one-half lines of dots. We will not follow the posthumous martyrology of the stanza, with its distorted, supplemented, and at last "restored" study of Pushkin. We also will not conjecture that Pushkin omitted the lines because of their unprintability, for then he could have eliminated only the last two lines, or the entire stanza. In a word, the unprintability of a single line could not have an effect on all the variations of omissions which Pushkin created several times. We also will not conjecture that Pushkin omitted the stanza because of its inartistic quality, for there is nothing which indicates this. What is interesting to us is the fact that Pushkin omitted lines, having retained the first phrase, and in place of four and one-half lines of text, placed three and one half lines of dots. In the second case, having given two lines of text, he then placed two lines of dots in place of three missing lines.

What was the result of this? Pushkin achieved a similarity of stanzas, subtly consistent. The entire poem consists of fifteen stanzas. Only two of them (excluding the one being examined) have five lines, and these two stanzas are at a distance of six stanzas from ours. Besides, it would not do to forget that the four-line stanza is a common, typical stanza, the stanza *par excellence*. Four lines, out of which three and one-half are dots, serve as an *equivalent* of the stanza, *for which Pushkin quite obviously did not give indications as to a definite omission*. (Otherwise he would have filled in the corresponding number of lines with dots.)[20] Only a segment of the first line here proves to have sound and significance.

The dots here do not even remotely allude to the semantics of the

43

text or its phonation, but they nevertheless give quite enough to become an *equivalent of the text*. The given *meter* (with a shaped momentum) is in definite stanzaic arrangement. Although the metrical unity does not nearly coincide with the syntactical unity, and because of this the quality of the syntax is never indicated, the somewhat typical form is able to stand at a distance from and to stabilize distributions of syntax in the stanza as a result of the preceding text. Consequently, perhaps here we have a hint as to the quantity of the syntactic parts. Consider Potebnia:

> According to the quantity of parts of a musical period,
> one can judge as to the quantity of the syntactical parts
> of the measure. To guess, however, at what precisely the
> latter consists of is impossible. For example, the same mu-
> sical phrase corresponds in one case to an attribute and to the
> attributed—chervonaia kalyon'ka ("red berry"), and in another
> to an adverb and that which is subject to it plus a predicate—
> tam divchyna zhurylasia ("there a girl grieved"). An exact
> correspondence of melody and lexical significances of song
> is impossible.[21]

This is not a result, of course, of the consecutive reunification and articulation of metrical features, nor of their unification in the full sense of the word. The meter is given as a sign, as an almost partially-hidden *potential*. Before us, however, is the sign of the equality of the segment and of the dots with an entire stanza, allowing us to regard the line of the following stanza ("Proshchai zhe more") ("Farewell then, sea") precisely as part of the *following* stanza. In the segment between the beginning of the stanza and the beginning of the next stanza is the *flow of a stanza*, and the metrical energy of an entire stanza is communicated to the segment. Thus the meaningful validity of the equivalent is revealed. Before us in an uncertain text (the uncertainty of which, however, is quite limited and semi-revealed), but the role of an uncertain text (of *any* test in the semantic aspect), instilled into the continuous construction of verse, is immeasurably greater than the role of a definite text. The feature of this partial uncertainty is filled. with the maximum tension of the missing elements, of that which is potentially given. Above all, it makes the developing form dynamic.

This is why the phenomenon of equivalents does not signify a lowering or a weakening, but rather the pressure and tension of unspent, dynamic elements.

Thus is made clear the distinction (of the equivalent) from a *pause*. A pause is a homogeneous element of speech, not interceding in any area besides its own, whereas in the equivalent we have something with a heterogeneous element, distinguished by its very functions from the elements in which it is instilled. This decides the question in the acoustic approach to verse about the lack of convergence in the equivalent. *Acoustically, we do not reproduce the equivalent. Only the pause is reproduced.* However the pause would set off the empty space, the segment remains a *segment*. The pause does not designate a stanza, but remains a *pause*, not interceding in any space, let alone the fact that it is powerless to express quantity of metrical periods, and, along with this, the constructive role of the equivalent. The example introduced, however, is not isolated or accidental. I will introduce several more examples. The role of the "equivalent" is quite appreciable in verse. "The Motionless Guard" ("Nedvizhnyi strazh," 1823), is written in the canonical stanzaic form of the ode.[22]

In the third stanza of the ode, in the clear hand of Pushkin, there are three lines of dots in place of four missing lines.[23]

The stanza reads as such:

> "Svershilos', " molvil on. Davno l' narody mira
> Paden'e slavili velikogo kumira,
> . . . .
> . . . .
> . . . .
>
> "It has happened," he said. Was it long ago the
>   people of the world
> Celebrated the downfall of a great idol,
> . . . .
> . . . .

One must call to mind the strength of metrical habit which was a result of a canonical, complex, and closed stanza in order to value the force of the equivalent, which breaks up the automatism of the meter.

In the poem "The Captain" ("Polkovodets"), Pushkin includes the following equivalent of the text:

> Tam, ustarelyi vozhd', kak ratnik molodoi,
> Svintsa veselyi svist zaslyshavshii vpervoi,
> Brosalsia ty v ogon', ishcha zhelannoi smerti–
> Votshche!–
> . . . .
> . . . .
> O liudi! Zhalkii rod, dostoinyi slez i smekha!
> Zhretsy minutnogo poklonnika uspekha, i.t.d.
>
> There, an antiquated leader, like a young warrior,
> Leaden the merry whistle once heard,

45

You threw yourself into the fire, seeking the longed-for death—
In vain!
. . . .
. . . .
Oh people! A wretched sort, deserving of tears and laughter!
Priests of a momentary worshipper of success, etc.

(Again, such references to "incompleteness" do not explain anything, and are intolerable in relationship to the things presented as "incomplete" by the author himself. "Incompleteness" here becomes an aesthetic fact, and we must regard the dots not from the point of view of "omitted," but from the point of view of an "absence.")

Thus, in this stanza Pushkin: (a) singled out the segment "Votshche" ("in vain") and the *pause*, as if filling in the first verse by having left an empty place, (b) gave an equivalent of the stanza. The former gave him the chance to single out the segment with unusual force, while the latter is a fact of construction. Here, the insufficiency of the acoustic approach in the case of equivalents comes even more clearly into view. Having emphasized the *segment* and the *pause* within it, there is no way to set off the *stanzaic equivalent*.

The artistic significance of the "extract" and the "fragment" as a genre is partly based, perhaps, on the dynamic significance of the equivalent. Consider "The Cloudy Day Has Faded Out" ("Nenastnyi den' potukh"), printed by Pushkin under the title of "Fragment":

> *Odna...Ni ch'im ustam ona ne predaet*
> *Ni plech, ni vlazhnykh ust, ni persei belosnezhnykh*
> . . . .
> . . . .
> . . . .
> *Nikto ee liubvi nebesnoi nedostoin.*
> *Nepravda l': ty odna? ty plachesh? Ia spokoen;*
> . . . .
> *No esli . . . .* [24]

Alone... She does not give to anyone's lips
Her shoulder, nor moist lips, nor snowy breast
. . . .
. . . .
. . . .
No one is worthy of her divine love.
It isn't true: you alone? you crying? I am at peace;
. . . .
But if. . . . .

46

The nature of the so-called "omitted stanzas" is much more complex in *Eugene Onegin*, on which there is no space to dwell upon in detail here. This case is especially interesting, for in relationship to it, it is definitely established that: (1) partial absences of the text are called for exclusively by internal, constructive motives, and that, (2) the marks are not signs of definite omissions, and often do not signify any definite text. ("The absence of unwritten stanzas," according to the quite unsuccessful formulation of M. Hoffman.)

Here we meet a partial absence of the text inside the stanza-chapter, which suits those cases mentioned above, and the use of dynamic markings instead of an *entire* stanza-chapter (ciphers). These dynamic markings have a double significance: they appear as stanzaic and plot-line equivalents. Here the principle of the *stanza* plays its own role. In the stanza as a unity, the quantity of metricosyntactic periods is more or less planned. In this way, the mark plays the role of verse. This role significantly complicates the second purpose—to be a sign of the link of the plot, a type of *false time* of the plot. This complexity and duality is based on the complexity of *Eugene Onegin* as a "novel in verse."

Equivalents, as I have indicated, do not signify a weakening, a lowering or a rest in the process of the developing form, but, on the contrary, signify pressure and amplification.

This is based, by the way, on the following fact. The dynamic of form is a continuous violation of automatism, a continuous pushing forward of the constructive factor and the deformation of the subordinated factors. The antinomy of form in a given case consists of the following. The very continuity of interaction (of struggle) automatizes form by the monotony of its flow. Therefore, an alteration in the ratio between the constructive factors and all others is one of the unquestionable demands of dynamic form. From this point of view, form is the continuous arrangement of diverse equivalents, heightening the dynamism. Thus, the *material* may be altered to the *minimum amount necessary to still be a sign of the constructive principle*. Similar to the way in which a tag with the inscription "forest" was sufficient in depicting the forest in the medieval theater, in poetry a tag of any element is sufficient in place of the element itself. We even take the number of a stanza as the stanza itself, and, as we saw, it is constructively equal with the stanza itself. Thus, the equivalent, flowing along the qualitatively altered material, reveals the constructive principle with the greatest force. In the examples introduced, the metrical side of verse is revealed.[25]

5. Meter and Rhythm

If the example of equivalents of a text shows the *irreducability* of verse to the acoustic approach, then others will show the superfluous element which is brought to verse by the acoustic approach.

One of the great merits of *Ohrenphilologie* is its broadening of the concept of rhythm. Let us examine, however, the content and volume of this concept of rhythm which flows consistently from the acoustic approach.[26] According to Saran (in his early work), the factors of rhythm are:

> 1) meter, that is, the firm relations in which duration
> *(Dauerwerte)* is located, in which diverse categories of
> sound and sound groupings combine with each other.
> Thus, meter is a mathematical concept of the firm
> relationships of duration in the movement of sounds.
> This concept should not be confused with rhythm. 2)
> dynamics, that is, the concept of the gradation of strength
> *(Stärkeabstufungen)*, marking the ranks of sounds. 3) pace
> 4) agogics, that is, the little lengthenings and shortenings
> which the normal duration of a unit *(eines Wertes)* under-
> goes, without disturbing the awareness of basic proportions.
> 5) sound articulation (legato, staccato, and so on). 6) the
> dead pause, that is, irrational, empty time used in the
> capacity of partitioning. 7) melody, with its significant
> intervals and interferences. 8) the text, which with its syntactic
> divisions and shift of accented and unaccented syllables,
> essentially promotes the formation of rhythmical groups.
> 9) euphony of the text, for example, rhyme, alliteration,
> and so on, on which rhythm is also based.

Such a definition of the volume of rhythm is undoubtedly too broad. (Incidentally, the formless term "text" calls forth the objection. The syntactical connections of the text are undoubtedly the significant factor in the interation of factors which generate rhythm; but the shift of accented and unaccented syllables of the text as a whole enters into the concept of meter.) What is extremely curious is the confusion of *the acoustic and the articulatory* points of view in the concept of the "gradation of strength," which is retained by Saran even later.[27] But a much greater doubt is called forth by the rhythmical function of agogics, the small lengthenings and shortenings of the normal duration of the unity *which do not disturb the consciousness of basic proportions.* Here the factors of rhythm are improperly broadened by the consistent acoustic approach. These small alterations, not disturbing the consciousness of basic proportion, are significant only as properties of the acoustic feature, and quite obviously not as factors of rhythm. However, this broadening is not accidental. The excessive breadth of volume in the concept of rhythm leads to a corresponding narrowness in the definition of the content of the concept: "Rhythm is the aesthetically pleasing form of a preceding acoustic feature."[28]

I will not speak about the coarsely hedonistic side of the definition, which is retained even later by Saran. The principal narrowed feature in the given definition is the attachment of rhythm to the acoustic feature, and regarding it as an acoustic system.

On the question of the interaction of factors, Saran notes:

> Only the combined action of all or almost all factors est-
> ablishes rhythm. They need not, however, act in one and the
> same direction. Some may even act in a contrary way;
> they must be compensated for by the greater strength of
> action of the others. In such cases—and they are quite com-
> mon—the ideal rhythmical system is more or less obscured
> *(verschleiert)*. It is precisely in the delicate usage of con-
> trary factors that the art of rhythmical creation is con-
> tained.[29]

Without a doubt, such are the *maximal* conditions of rhythm, but there still remains the question: what are the minimal conditions?

The minimal conditions of rhythm are such that the factors whose interaction generate it are not given the aspect of a system, but the aspect of a *sign* of a system. In this way, rhythm may be given the aspect of a sign of rhythm, which simultaneously appears as a sign of meter, a necessary factor of rhythm, the dynamic grouping of material. Thus, meter as a regular accentual system may be absent. The basis of meter lies not so much in the presence of a system, as in the presence of its principle. The principle of meter consists of the dynamic grouping of vocal material according to an accentual indication. The most simple and basic phenomenon here will be the isolation of some metrical group as a *unit*. This isolation is simultaneously a dynamic preparation for the following, similar (not identical, but similar) group. If this metrical preparation is allowed, we have before us a metrical system. Metrical grouping follows the path of (1) dynamically-successive metrical preparation, and (2) dynamically-simultaneous metrical allowance, uniting metrical unities into higher groups—metrical wholes. The first, in and of itself, will be a progressive motor force of grouping, while the second will be regressive. Preparation and allowance (and also unification) may be total, breaking up unities into pieces (*Abschnitt*, or stops). They may lead to even higher groups and result in the realization of *metrical form* (the sonnet, the rondeau, etc., as metrical forms). This progressive-regressive rhythmical property of meter is one of the reasons why it is a *major* component of rhythm. In instrumentation we have only the regressive feature. However, although the concept of rhyme contains both features, it already assumes the availability of a metrical series.

But what if the dynamic preparation is not allowed in the following similar group? In such a case, meter ceases to exist in the shape of a regular system, but it does exist in another way. "Prohibited preparation" is also a feature which creates dynamism. Meter is retained in the shape of a metrical impulse; thus, every "prohibition" results in a metrical regrouping. We have either a coordination of unities (which is accomplished progressively), or a subordination (which is accomplished regressively). Such verse will metrically be free verse, *vers libre, vers irregulier*. Here meter as a dynamic principle replaces meter as a system. Properly speaking, we have orientation toward meter, the equivalent of meter.

Therefore, the concept of *verse unity* receives quite an exceptional significance here, along with the feature of its isolation. The graphic plays a special role here, drawing signs of metrical unity together with the sign of rhythm. The graphic here becomes a signal of verse, of rhythm. Just as in systematic verse there exists, as a measure, a small unity isolated from the series, so here the basic measure is the series itself. Dynamic preparation is applied to it as a whole, and the prohibiting of it in the following verse series is a feature which also makes the series dynamic as a whole. (The possibility of *vers libre* as a blending of systematic verses is not ruled out, but precisely the blending of various systems. Here all are equal in view of this integral prohibition. The criterion will be the entire series—not the first one, of course, but each one previous to it.)

Thus, *vers libre* presents itself as a "variable" of metrical form. The important significance of unity compels us to impart an important role to the syntactical articulations occurring here. Nevertheless, I cannot agree with the formulation of V. M. Zhirmunsky: "The regulation of the syntactical structure constitutes the basis of the compositional articulation of free verse."[30] In the first place, not all forms of free verse approach this concept of *regulation* of their syntactical structure (consider Mayakovsky). In the second place, the important significance in *vers libre* of the factor of syntactical articulations must not cover up the feature of meter as a dynamic principle. It is interesting to compare the opinion of Wundt on ancient European poetry, where syntactical articulations play, as is known, an unusually important role: "Here, as everywhere, *parallelismus membrorum* does not replace rhythm, as was earlier supposed, but accompanies it as an amplification, which develops on its foundation and supposes its presence."[31]

Thus, it is easily observed that as regularity of a metrical system— a too cheaply achieved license—leads quite quickly to automatism of verse, the feature of the metrical equivalent makes it dynamic.

And so, what defines verse in the given case is not the systematic

50

interaction of rhythm (the maximal conditions), but the orientation toward a system—its principle (the minimal conditions). It is all the same whether a systematic group is *given* us, or whether we only strive toward it, and in striving, we create the grouping *sui generis*. The result is speech which has been made dynamic. Since it is the sign which proves to be important in the concept of *verse*, the principle which makes it dynamic, and not its mode of construction, we see revealed here the quite rich area of the creation of equivalents. In an epoch when traditional meter is not in the condition to build the dynamism of the material, since its bond with the material has become automatic, there ensues an epoch of equivalents.

In our own time *vers libre* has gained great victories. It is time to say that it is the characteristic verse of our epoch, and to relate to it as to something exceptional, or even as verse on the border of prose, is as incorrect historically as it is theoretically.

Vers libre properly occurs by the consistent utilization of the principle of "prohibition of dynamic preparation," carried out on metrical unities. Other metrical organizations use the principle of "prohibition" partially, on smaller metrical sections. After the isolation of a metrical unity follows the isolation of smaller metrical units inside unities, which lays the foundation for the further flow of meter. Systematic verse is thus based on the isolation of smaller units. Each partial prohibition of preparation of this small unity makes systematic verse dynamic. Here are the roots of the phenomenon of the so-called "pauznik," in which there is no pause, but there is the feature of the partial prohibition of preparation.

The appearance of *vers libre* in Russia apparently goes back to the sixties, and is connected with the names of Fet and Polonsky. (Consider the parody of Turgenev in 1859.) Its roots and embryo however, one can see in Zhukovsky ("Rustem i Zorab": the absence of rhyme and the irregular alternation of iambic tetrameter, iambic trimeter, and iambic pentameter as an orientation toward quantitative prohibition). The "pauznik" in the broad sense of the word appears in the end of the 18th century and develops in the beginning of the 19th century (Burinsky, 1804; Zhukovsky, 1818). It is curious that in the thirties, when the exhaustion of systematic verse (especially iambic tetrameter) was sensed quite sharply, there were attempts to substantiate the "pauznik." Consider the article "On Italian Versification,"[32] where the engagement of the "Italian blank note" and the "pause" is advocated: "As in music," writes the author, "a note is often replaced by time (by tempo) and a halt which is called a pause, so in the Italian foot, the measure is often supplemented with a suspension, which is called a pause." At this point the author adds a footnote:

In ancient Russian songs the pause is met quite frequently.
It is a pity that Lomonosov, the compiler of our rules of

51

versificàtion, did not turn his attention to this. With
the pause it would be easier for us in a translation of
Italian poets to retain the musicality of their verses."

6. Equivalents of the Text

We observe the phenomenon of the creation of equivalents in other
factors of rhythm also. I will indicate here some equivalents of rhyme.

S. I. Bernshtein, in the interesting article "On the Methodological
Significance of the Phonetic Study of Rhymes,"[33] comes to the conclusion that "inexact" rhymes break down into two categories. In the first
are placed inexact rhymes which are used as an acoustically-effective device.
The inexact rhyme indeed may be an effective device acoustically. Here the
imperfect identity of the rhyming members as an intensifying feature plays
its own role. Let us remember that the paling of the acoustic feature, observed in the Karamzinian epoch, was simultaneously accompanied by a struggle
with the "ringing of inexact rhymes" and the introduction of exact rhymes.
The ode of the 18th century—the form of oratorical poetry in which the
acoustic feature *eo ipso* was quite essential—was connected in the literary
consciousness of Derzhavin with inexact rhyme, apparently as being more
valid acoustically.[34] But another type of inexact rhyme is the "equivalent"
of exact rhyme, in which the disparity between the phonic "plan" of poetry
and the material of its phonation arises.[35]

Here is a type of "equivalent" of exact rhyme. We have here a failure
of the "phonated" plan to converge not so much with the material sound,
as with the acoustic side of this sound.

It is possible to point out other examples which, although appearing
to be equivalents of rhymes, will not rhyme by the acoustic approach.
Such are *remote* rhymes. Let us take the following stanza of Tiutchev:

1. *Konchen pir, umolkli khory,*
2. *Oporozheny amfory,*
3. *Oprokinuty korziny,*
4. *Ne dopity v kubkakh viny,*
5. *Na glavakh venki izmiaty;*
6. *Lish' kurilis' aromaty*
7. *V opustevshei svetloi zale.*
8. *Konchiv pir, my pozdno vstali:*
9. *Zvezdy na nebe siiali,*
10. *Noch' dostigla poloviny.*

1. The feast is done, the choruses are silent,
2. The amphora is empty,

52

3. The baskets overturned,
4. The wine not drunk in the goblets,
5. On heads wreaths are crumpled;
6. Only the fragrances smoking
7. In the deserted and lighted hall.
8. Having finished the feast, we rose late:
9. The stars shone in the sky,
10. It was already past midnight...

The final, tenth line rhymes with lines three and four, at a distance of five lines.

In rhyme, as in the factor of rhythm, we observe two features—a progressive feature (the first rhymed member) and a regressive feature (the second rhymed member). Rhyme, as is meter, is a result of dynamic, progressive preparation and dynamic, regressive license. Thus, rhyme proves to be dependent on the strength of the progressive feature to an equal or even greater extent than on the strength of the regressive one. The dependence of rhyme on many factors—in the first place, on syntax—is based on this. The third and fourth rhyming lines present themselves as *completed* clauses:

3. *Oprokinuty korziny,*
4. *Ne dopity v kubkakh viny.*

3. The baskets overturned,
4. The wine not drunk in the goblets.

Therefore, their equally *progressive* strength comes to naught (also owing to the rhymed momentum AB-AB). This is why the rhyme with the tenth line is so weakly sensed.[36]

And so, in the complete absence of the progressive feature, in the case examined we have only the regressive feature of the relation of the word (and also of the metrical series) to a previous group. Nevertheless, this regressive feature may be so strong as to create rhyme. Here, however, the acoustic approach proves to be insufficient. The "rhyme" before us is almost not sensed acoustically across the distance of the rhymed members.

Speaking of instrumentation, it would not do to speak of its equivalents as a sign. Meter and rhyme, as rhythmical factors, have two dynamic features: the progressive and the regressive. Thus, the progressive feature will be the equivalent of meter (with the comparatively secondary significance of the regressive); the regressive feature will be the equivalent of rhyme (with the comparatively secondary significance of the progressive). But the concept of "instrumentation" does not at all contain, or only contains to the minimal degree, the progressive feature. Sounds do not assume what follows, whether identical or similar. Each phonation similar to a previous one unites into groups via a regressive path.[37]

Equivalents of meter and rhyme are inexpressible in the acoustic approach. Here *vers libre* comes together with rhythmical prose, and the remote rhyme disappears. This, along with everything else, must be recognized as a device, and not as the falling-out of a system.

By the very fact of equivalents of a text, one can be convinced that to proceed from the *word* as an indivisible, inseparable element of verbal art, to regard it as "the brick from which the building is constructed" will not do. We apportion this element with much more subtle "verbal elements."[38]

7. The Function of Rhythm in Verse and Prose

The concept of rhythm as a system, taken outside of its functional role, is in general possible only as a pre-condition of rhythm in its function, i.e., rhythm viewed as a constructive factor. It has been established for quite a while now that artistic prose is not an indifferent, unorganized mass in relationship to rhythm as a system. On the contrary, one may boldly assert that the question concerning the phonetic organization of prose occupied and occupies a place not smaller (although different) than the question of phonetic organization in poetry. Beginning with Lomonosov, Russian prose has undergone phonetic treatment. (Lomonosov had the greatest oratorical influence with regard to this issue. Consider the chapter from *Rhetoric*, "On the Flow of the Word," which is entirely given over to prose, presenting a number of obligatory rhythmical and euphonic instructions.)[39]

Every revolution in prose is perceived as a revolution in the phonetic composition of prose. Here it is interesting to recall the remark of Shevyrev that the folk song, with its dactylic endings, had an influence on the prose of Karamzin, having determined its dactylic clauses. This remark, of course, needs verification.[40]

At times (in particular, during a period of the rapprochment of prose and poetry) poetry most likely has been able to borrow certain phonetic devices from prose. The same Shevyrev writes about Pushkin: "From the thick solution of Karamzinian speech, strengthened with our ancient words, he forged his bronzed iambic pentameter, the marvelous form of Russian drama."[41]

No one can doubt that the prose of Flaubert and Turgenev is more "musical" (even more "rhythmical") than *vers libre*.[42]

The latest stages of Russian prose and poetry seem as if they have agreed to exchange "rhythmicalness" and even "metricality." While the prose of A. Bely is "metrical" throughout, many of his verses draw upon sources from outside metrical systems.

This corresponds with a great number of naive attempts in different languages to sweep away the boundaries between prose and *vers libre*, i.e., verse. The experiments of Guyau on the metrical articulation of Rabelais, Zola, and others are known. Regarding the *vers libre* of Rene and Souza, Grammont writes:

> These verses can not properly be considered as "rhymed."
> They would perhaps then be considered "verses"; however,
> these verses had nothing to distinguish them from rhythmical
> prose. Such are the phrases of Flaubert which we come across
> in *Bouvard et Pécuchet...* All that would distinguish this
> poetry from this prose was that Flaubert preceded and fol-
> lowed his short phrases with phrases which were distinct
> according to their rhythm. In the poetry, each piece would
> be rhythmically monotonous.[43]

He goes on to compare the verse of Viele-Griffin and Gustave Kahn with passages not only from Flaubert's *Bouvard et Pécuchet* and *Salammbo,* but also from Zola's *Germinal.* Here he refers to Guyau, who in a similar manner worked even earlier with the last two passages.

An investigator of Heine, Jules Legras, writes about the *freie Rhythmen* in "The North Sea" ("Nordsee"):

> It is not known whether Heine himself looked on this
> *vers libre* as he looked on verse. It should be noted that
> we would have been able to write these verses without any
> difficulty in a line, as prose is written. Heine without a
> doubt would willingly have agreed with this. It is very
> likely that this rhythmical prose came into existence
> under the influence of the rhythmical prose of Novalis.[44]

(It remains to be wondered at how Heine himself felt about this, since he did not write "The North Sea" ("Nordsee") in linear form. If Heine was quite indifferent to whether this was verse or prose, as Legras feels, we would not have this *freie Rhythmen.* As we see, this question is easily decided.)

In Russia, we have the well known experiments of Bely, Grossman, Shengeli, N. Engel'gardt, and others working in this direction.

This problem is, of course, easy to solve. This is especially the case since the refined, phonetic organization of prose is beyond doubt.

Let us compare the prose of Andrei Bely (*Ofeira,* for example or *Epopeia*) with the *vers libre* of Nel'dikhen. Bely's prose is much more "metrical" than these verses, and more tightly organized in euphonic terms.

Tredyakovsky had already gone quite a long way in the definition of *specificity of verse* outside the signs of verse systems. Consider "The Method of Verse Composition":

2. All that verse has in common with prose does not distinguish one from the other. Besides this, the letters, syllables, the accent of stress (which is given only once in any word and on one syllable), as well as the very words themselves, the segments of the periods, and the periods in general of both prose and verse, cannot be used to distinguish between prose and verse.
3. The definite number of syllables... does not distinguish verse from prose, for the segments of the so-called rhetorical isocolon also have an almost definite number, yet these segments are not verses.
5. Rhyme... in the same manner does not distinguish verse from prose, for rhyme cannot be rhyme without joining one verse line to another, i.e., rhyme cannot occur without two lines of verse. (However, each line alone and in and of itself must be verse.)

7. The elevation of style, the boldness of images, the liveliness of the figures of speech, the rushing movement, the abrupt ending of a sequence, and so on, do not distinguish verse from prose, for all of these are at times used by rhetoricians and historians.[45]

To a considerable degree, these lines have not become obsolete even up to the present day. To them we need only add "metricality." A comparison of the prose of Bely and *vers libre* is sufficient to convince us that from now on even the accentual system is not a specific and sufficient sign of verse (although the accentual principle remains a necessary corollary of verse construction). If we consider as verses those lines without the graphic sign of verse arrangement, then these are usually lines with a maximum of fulfilled conditions, which already have been crystallized into a system in a certain way. It is worth comparing this maximum of fulfilled conditions with the minimum of fulfilled conditions. This minimum of conditions is a sign which determines that verse is not in some system, but in those conditions which give us the sign of verse. *Vers libre* may be called prose only within polemical articles, while nobody considers the prose of Bely as verses.

No matter how much phonic, in the broad sense of the word, organization accompanies prose, it does not result in prose becoming verse. On the other hand, however closely verse approaches prose in this regard, it will never become prose.

This is precisely the *raison d'etre* that "rhythmical prose" exists within the prosaic series, and *vers libre* exists within the verse series. (If we were to set a good part of our *vers libre* into prose, hardly anyone would be able to read it.) The "poem in prose" as a genre, and the "novel in verse" as a genre are based on the disparity between their respective phenomena,

56

and not on their proximity. The "poem in prose" always reveals the essence of prose, while the "novel in verse" reveals the essence of verse: "I write not a novel, but a *novel in verse*—a devilish difference"(Pushkin). Thus, the distinction between verse and prose as being systematic and unsystematic in the phonic relationship to speech is refuted by the facts themselves. The distinction is located in the area of the *functional role of rhythm*. It is precisely this functional role of rhythm which is decisive, and not the systems in which it is presented.

What would be the result if we were to write *vers libre* as prose?

There are two possible outcomes: either the verse articulations of *vers libre* will coincide with the syntactic articulations, or they will not coincide. We will examine the latter of these two first. Here the verse unity is not covered by the syntactico-semantic unity of the verse graphic. If the divisions are not emphasized and not connected by rhymes, they are joined in the prosaic configuration. Thus, we destroy the *unity of the verse series.* Simultaneously with the unity another sign is destroyed—the compact connections in which verse unity places the words united within it. The compactness of the verse series collapses. *But it is precisely the unity and compactness of the series which is the objective sign of verse rhythm.* Both signs are to be found in intimate connection with each other. The concept of compactness may well assume the presence of the concept of unity. Even the unity is found to be dependent upon the compactness of series of vocal material. This is why the quantitative content of the verse series is limited. If the unity is quantitatively too broad, it either loses its own boundaries or is itself broken up into unities, i.e., it ceases in both cases to be unified. Both of these signs—the unity and the compactness of the verse series—create a third distinctive sign: *the dynamization of the vocal material.* The unified and compact vocal series here is more united and restrained than in conversational speech. In being unwound, the poem necessarily detaches the *verse unit.* We have seen that in systematic verse a part of the series will be such a unit, such as a halt (*Abschnitt*), or even a foot. In *vers libre* such a unit is altered. The unit serves each previous series in relationship to the next. Thus, the dynamics of the vocal material in systematic verse proceeds by means of the principle of isolation of this small unit. Its dynamic in *vers libre* proceeds by means of the fact that each series is recognized as the criterion (sometimes with the partial isolation of a small metrical unit, which meets, however, with a rebuff in the following line, without breaking up the unit). In the case of *systematic verse*, therefore, we have *words* being made dynamic. Each word serves simultaneously as an object of several vocal categories (the vocal word—the metrical word). With *vers libre* we usually have groups being made dynamic (for these same reasons), since the detached word is able to represent a group (cf. Mayakovsky). Thus, the unity and the compactness of the verse series regroup the syntactico-semantic connections and articulations. (In the case of the coinciding of the verse series with the grammatical unity, they deepen and emphasize the features of the syntactico-semantic connections and articulations.) This dynamization of vocal material draws a sharp boundary between the verse word and the prosaic word. The system of interaction between the tendencies of the verse series and the tendencies of the grammatical unity, the tendencies of the verse stanza and the grammatical whole, of the vocal word and the metrical word, acquires a decisive role. The word proves to be a compromise, *the result of two series.* The same is true of the clause. Consequently, the word proves to be *impeded*, while the vocal process is *successive.* This is in keeping with the example of the poet's consciousness of the role of meter as impeding speech. (See note no. 38.)

Practical speech (in the ideal) is characterized by the feature of the *simultaneity* of vocal groups (or more correctly, the aspiration toward it). This determines the relative significance of features of the outward sign ("Not parts, but signs") ("Nicht Teile, sondern Merkmale")—Wundt. Consider Shcherba's *Russkie glasnye (Russian Vowels)*, and also L. P. Yakubinsky and Viktor Shklovsky. (Here, incidentally, the bankruptcy of relating toward poetic language as a special dialect becomes clear. In not one dialect are there any particular conditions which are produced linguistically by *construction*.)

We know the subjective conditions in which semantic presentations play an insignificant role. The center of gravity accordingly turns to the successive features of speech (i.e., Wundt's "parts." Consider Benno Erdmann, and L. P. Yakubinsky's article in "The Book Corner.") In seeking a clue to subjective linguistic conditions, there is no need to present poetry (or more correctly, and more narrowly, verse) as a phenomenon of such a type, or to connect it with phenomena deviating from normal vocal occurrences. We should look into the objective conditions of verse as a construction, to which is related the dynamics of speech as a result of the application of basic principles of verse—the unity and compactness of the verse series—to the unwinding of verse material. The obscuring and insignificance of the semantic element is not typical here, but rather its *subordination* to the feature of rhythm: its *deformation.*

Therefore, if we were to reproduce *vers libre* as prose, in which the verse series is not covered syntactically, we would disturb the unity and compactness of the verse series, and deprive it of the dynamics of speech. Here the constructive principle of prose advances. The verse connections and articulations are eliminated, and in their place we see syntactico-semantic connections and articulations.

Let us now reproduce *vers libre* as prose, in which the verse series coincides with the grammatical unity (or whole). The unity of the verse series is destroyed, but the syntactical unity coinciding with it remains. The feature of the compactness of the verse series will fall away, but the essential connection between the members of the syntactic unity remains.

58

Every transmission to prose will destroy the verse, for *the feature of vocal dynamics falls away.* Although the verse series does not completely lose its own boundaries, it will no longer be verse. In the unwinding of the material, neither the verse measure nor unit is bared. At the same time, the dynamization of the word and of verbal groups falls away, which results in the falling away of the successive nature of the word in verse.

At this subtle boundary, however, it is made clear that on one hand rhythm is still an insufficient definition of the constructive principle of verse, and an insufficient characterization of verse speech, guided by the outward sign of the word. On the other hand the definition of the constructive principle of prose as a simultaneous utilization of the semantic elements of the word is insufficient.

The heart of the matter lies in the *subordination* of one feature to another. It lies in the *deforming influence* in which the principle of rhythm joins with the principle of the simultaneous reunion of vocal elements (of verbal groups and words) in verse. The exact opposite is true in prose. Therefore, the "rhythm of prose" is functionally remote from the "rhythm of verse." These are two different phenomena.

The constructive principle of any series has assimilative strength. It subordinates and deforms the phenomena of another series. This is why "rhythmicalness" is not rhythm, and *"metricalness"* is not meter. Rhythm in prose is assimilated by the constructive principle of prose, by the predominance in it of the semantic purpose of speech. This rhythm can play a communicative role, or a positive role (emphasizing and reinforcing the syntactico-semantic unity), or a negative role (fulfilling the role of counterattraction or deflection). Too strong a "rhythmicalness" of prose, therefore, has brought upon itself, at various times and in various literatures, reproaches. Not becoming "rhythm," rhythmicalness has interfered. Jean-Paul wrote:

> It is remarkable that resounding euphony can prevent comprehension, not in poetry, but in prose. This is all the more true in the presence of images, for images present ideas, but harmony only accompanies them. However, this can only happen when the ideas are insufficiently great and powerful, so that we are excited and held continually by the sensation and examination of their signs, i.e., the sounds. The greater the strength in the work, the more it allows us to endure their ringing. The echo occurs in large halls, and not in a room.[46]

Here it excellently noted that rhythm, being the constructive factor of verse (according to Jean-Paul "expressing and presenting ideas"), is not able to interfere in verse. The exact opposite occurs in prose, where it is sometimes a distracting, interfering feature. I. Martynov wrote at the beginning of the 19th century:

Prose must be like prose. It has the right to command words, and to place them anywhere they are necessary, as long as they have their effect and strength. Any measure in it is unbearable. This can be seen by the fact that a good writer will go to great lengths to be careful that his writing does not have any expressions which resemble verse. And, if by chance we find in some prose the measure of verses, then it brings upon itself a certain repugnance.[47]

Of course, "repugnance" is characteristic evidence of the epoch, since it is not obligatory. This characteristic evidence, however, shows a clear awareness of the specificity of the prosaic construction. The problem naturally arises as following. One should judge rhythm in prose from the point of view of prosaic construction, and consider the functional role of rhythm here. I will cite the typical opinion of L. Trotsky concerning the rhythm of A. Bely's prose. From this viewpoint, prosaic rhythm resembles a flapping shutter on a sleepless night: you wait to be sure that it will flap. The "flapping shutter" is a feature of the division of unities. It is necessary in successive verse speech as the basis of verse. Here the question of the consciousness of rhythm outside the material does not arise. As long as rhythm is the deciding, constructive basis of verse, its constructive "difficulty" cannot be a "hindrance."

Thus, before us are two closed constructive series: verse and prosaic. Each alteration within them is precisely an internal alteration. The orientation of verse in prose is the arrangement of the unity and the compactness of the verse series into an unusual object. Therefore, the essence of verse is not smoothed over, but on the contrary, is advanced with new strength. Thus, *vers libre*, the acknowledged "transition to prose," is an extraordinary advancement of the constructive verse principle, precisely because it is given in a foreign, unspecified object. Being inserted into the verse series, any element of prose is turned toward that side which is functionally advanced. This simultaneously creates two features: the emphasized feature of the construction—the feature of verse—and the feature of the deformation of the unusual object. The same is true for prose if the verse element is introduced into it. The definite, systematic character of prosaic clauses and of verse divisions between unities force the deformation of syntactico-semantic unities. Since inversions of an attribute and that which it defines (a device which has reached to our own day without any alteration) are weakly sensed at the end of a line precisely as inversions, every prosaic clause built on that inversion reveals above all its own syntactico-semantic side. This is why any rapprochment of prose with verse is in substance not a rapprochment, but the introduction of unusual material into a specific, closed construction.

As a consequence of what was said above, it is impossible to study the system of rhythm in prose and in verse in the same way, as these systems do not have anything in common with each other. In prose, we will have something totally inappropriate to verse rhythm, something functionally deformed by the general construction. Therefore, one cannot analyze the rhythm of prose and the rhythm of verse as phenomena which are equivalent to each other. In studying each, we should bear in mind their functional distinction.

But is not the situation the same with respect to semantic studies in verse? Since the principle of rhythm is deformed in prose, and rhythm is changed into "rhythmicalness," do we not have in verse a deformed semantics, which cannot be studied by abstracting speech from its constructive principle? And, in studying the semantics of the word in verse, having disregarded the verse, do we not make the very same mistake as the naive investigators who lightly and freely set the prose of Turgenev into verse, and the *freie Rhythmen* of Heine into prose?

8. Laws of Verse

Here we meet with an objection, which according to Meumann is formulated in the following way: rhythmicalized verbal material—*rhythmicalized material*—distracts from rhythm with its "sense." After what was said above, this is clearly an inherent contradiction of the very concept of *rhythmicalized material* with regard to verse. "Rhythm" and "material" are equated with two static systems, superimposed upon one another. Rhythm floats over the material, like oil over water. And, with complete consistency Meumann notes:

> ...The general tendency which prevents the advancement of rhythm in poetry is the following: rhythm may achieve an accessory effect (verse painting), where it receives a relatively independent significance on a level with the sense of verse. In a word, its advancement must always be motivated by special aesthetic effects.[48]

Thus, the duality of the constructive principle and the material is understood here not in the sense that the material has been subordinated to the principle, or arranged, or grouped according to it, or in short, deformed by it. Rather, it is understood in the sense that material exists independently from rhythm as the constructive principle. In turn, the constructive principle (rhythm) exists outside the material, adding to it from time to time "accessory effects." A. Schlegel has objected to such an understanding of "form and material" in his *Berlin Lectures (Berliner Vorlesungen.)* He writes the following concerning the form of the sonnet.

61

The opinion of those who maintain that the form of the sonnet imposes on the poet severe restrictions, that it is the procrustean bed on which they stretch or hem thought, does not even deserve an objection, for it applies equally to all versification. If this were so, one should consider every poem as an exercise which has first been written in formless prose and subsequently adjusted to verses according to the rules.[49]

Rhythmicalized material in essence is a fiction. In verse we do not face material which needs to be rhythmicalized, but rather material which already is rhythmicalized and deformed. It is not *rhythmicalized material,* but *material in rhythm.* It cannot "distract" from rhythm because it already has been exposed to its influence.

The question of the semantic element in verse is transferred to another plane. Where is the specificity of the verse word? What distinguishes *material in rhythm* from its prosaic double?

To many, the answer is suggested by the fact that the verse word is distinguished from the prosaic word by a special emotional coloring. This answer, however, touches upon the general question of the emotionality of art, a question which should not be raised or decided here. Concerning the specific question of the emotionality of the verse word, there is a consideration here which to a large extent deflects the question. The fact of the matter is that the concept of rhythm, the deciding factor in the present case, is not at all necessarily connected with emotionality. Meumann writes:

> The intellectual processes of rhythm are often present without any definite, accompanying emotion. (We group, subordinate, and inwardly make dynamic (*betonnen innerlich*) even in the presence of indifferent measures.) They are independent of emotional alterations. The greatest energy of internal connections is present precisely when (in the presence of slow rhythms) there is an extremely weak effect on the emotions.[50]

The concept of "artistic emotion" is a hybrid one, for it transfers the point of view of empirical emotions onto the concept of "artisticness." It awaits, however, the substantiation of this concept, and turns us once again to the facts of construction. We should look for our answer to this fascinating question in these facts and conditions of the construction.

It appears decisive in this situation that verbal presentations are members of rhythmical unities. These members prove to be in a stronger and more compact connection than in ordinary speech. Between the words arises a *correlation by position.* Consequently, one of the chief peculiarities here is the process of making the word dynamic, and therefore, its successiveness.

Thus, the factors of rhythm are:

1. the factor of the unity of the verse series;
2. the factor of its compactness;
3. the factor of the dynamization of vocal material, and
4. the factor of the successiveness of the vocal material in verse.

CHAPTER TWO

THE SENSE OF THE WORD IN VERSE

1. The Isolated Word and the Pure Lexical Word

A word does not have one definite meaning. It is a chameleon, in which not only various shades, but even various colors arise with each usage.

The abstraction of the "word" is, strictly speaking, a type of vessel, filled anew each time in dependence on the lexical structure in which it is placed, and on the functions which every vocal element carries. It is a type of cross section of these various lexical and functional structures.

Dualism in the definition of various trends of word-usages is normal. The "usual" and "occasional" meaning of Paul, "meaning" and "performance" according to Potebnia—these formulations of the question arise from the following dualism: the word outside the clause and the word in the clause. This is the same type of opposition we see in B. Erdmann's "Sachvorstellung" and "Bedeutungsvorstellung," in which the first corresponds to the meaning of the word in a clause, and the second to the meaning of the isolated word.[51]

The word does not exist outside of the clause. The isolated word does not stand in extra-phrasal conditions. It only is found in *other* conditions in comparison with the word in the clause. Pronouncing an isolated "dictionary" word, we do not obtain the "word in general," the pure, lexical word, but only the word in new conditions, in comparison with the conditions proposed by context. This is why semantic experiments with "words," in which isolated words are pronounced with the goal of stimulating in the listeners associative series, are experiments with worthless material, the results of which cannot be disseminated.

The terminological dualism noted above should be used in another way. Analyzing a series of word-usages, we encounter the phenomenon of the *unity of the lexical category*.

Let us take the "word" "earth."

1. Earth and Mars; earth and heaven (tellus).
2. To bury some object in the earth (humus).
3. He fell to earth (Boden).
4. Native earth (Land).

Without a doubt, we have before us various meanings of one "word" in assorted word-usages. Nevertheless, if we say of the Martian who falls onto the Martian Boden—"he fell to earth"—we feel the clumsiness, although "earth" in the complex "to fall to earth" is apparently quite far in meaning from "earth" in the previous complexes. It would also be clumsy to speak of the Martian soil as "gray earth."

What exactly is occurring here? What allowed us to consider these quite diverse usages as united, and to relate to them as to something which is each time identical? It is the presence of the category of lexical unity. This presence we shall call the *principal sign of meaning.*[52]

Why are we not able to speak in the given case about the Martian who fell to earth? Why is this word-usage not successful? It is because in speaking about the Martian, we were set in motion within a particular *lexical plan*:

> earth and Mars
> Black Earth
> he fell to earth
> native earth

Speaking of him, we proceeded to these various word usages from the first meaning, even when that meaning was something quite different. We have blended it in, for we were set in motion by a given lexical plan.

But this lexical plan became possible because the word "earth" was recognized each time as *indivisible.* In spite of the fact that each time it was made up of complex semantic overtones, *secondary signs,* and definite peculiarities of a given word-usage and a given lexical plan, the *principal sign* was present in it the entire time.

The unity of the lexical category (in other words, the presence of the principal sign of meaning) is revealed with great force upon the implementation of any word-usage.

A. Turgenev wrote to Prince Vyazemsky: "Instead of *protivnikov* (opponent), you always write *pobornikov*, but this means just the opposite, for the verb *poborat'* means: to promote, to help, to enable ('all prayers to our defenders and *pobornikam* of the heavenly powers')."[53] Prince Vyazemsky answered Turgenev:

> Of course you are right: *pobornik* was used by me incorrectly. *But in the sense of the language, it means that which I wish to express...* But you are incorrect when you say that the verb poborat' means "to promote." See the Academy Dictionary. Here we have "poborat' + accusative case" and "poborat' po + dative case": *"Poborokhom* the enemies of Israel" (Maccabees). And so, you are right, but I am not completely guilty. I confess that "protovnik" *is a word which is somewhat repulsive* ("protivnoe") *to me, but there is nothing I can do,* so I won't resist.[54]

Thus, Vyazemsky used the word *pobornik* instead of the word *protivnik*, and used it in quite the opposite meaning. Vyazemsky simultaneously realizes that "in the sense of the language" the word "means that which he wants to express," but the word "protivnik" is *repulsive* to him. How could this happen?

It happened for two reasons. The word *protivnik* is connected for Vyazemsky with the word "protivnyi," which has two meanings:

adversaire

"protivnyi"

rebutant

This was able to occur because the presence of the category of lexical unity (the principal sign) was recognized in the word "protivnyi." The word "protivnyi" was recognized as a unified lexical word. (If the category of unity were not here, if it had disintegrated and two principal signs had been formed, then Vyazemsky would not have found it difficult to connect the word "protivnik" with one meaning of the word "protivnyi.")

But why did Vyazemsky use the word "pobornik" instead of the word "protivnik"? Did not he himself recognize that the word "pobornik" is connected with the two meanings of the verb "poborat' "? The fact of the matter is that the lexical plan in which Vyazemsky moved could not endure the connections with the word "protivnyi" in its second meaning, and easily tolerated the connection with either meaning of the verb "poborat'." The lexical plan is made up of many conditions, which includes certain emotional colorations. The peculiar coloration of the type connected with the second meaning of the word "protivnyi" disturbed the coloring of the plan in which Vyazemsky moved (in the given case, the oratorical and the lofty), but the coloring of the word "poborat' " was quite suitable to him. We related this coloring to secondary signs.

Thus, the clumsiness of the usage of "protivnik" was based on the presence of the *principal sign,* while the choice of the word-usage depended on *secondary signs.*

The principal sign may be divided and multiplied, and the category of lexical unity may be violated.

Let us take the following example:

Priroda i Okhota (Nature and Hunting) (title of journal)
"U nego khot' priroda blagodarnaia, da okhoty u uchen'iu nikakoi."
"Although he has a noble nature, he has no inclination ("okhota") for studies."

Nothing compels us to consider the words "priroda" and "okhota" as identical or correlative in both phrases. Here there is no category of lexical unity, and the words in both cases are conveyed by quite different lexical plans.

Thus, there are generalizing lines of *unity*, owing to which the word is recognized as unified, in spite of its occasional alterations. Dualism may be considered as a fundamental division of the signs of meaning into two basic classes—the *principal* sign of meaning and *secondary* signs.

Here there should be a preliminary observation. The concept of the principal sign does not coincide with the concept of the material part of the word in the same manner as the concept of secondary signs does with the formal part. In the principal sign of the word "letaet" ("he, she, it flies"), the material characteristics and the formal maintain equality. In the phrases: "Man ("chelovek")—it rings proudly" and "Waiter ("chelovek"), a glass of tea," the formal and material sides of the word are equal, but the principal signs are different.[55]

Several examples of "secondary signs" are due.

Let us take the word "man" ("chelovek") in several of its usages:

1. "Man! It rings proudly. Man is you, I, he, man is not you, not I, not he... (M. Gorkii)

2. In high rank let him not forget/The holiest of callings: man. (Zhukovsky)

3. Yes, he was a man, on the entire earth
I will never find such a man. (Shakespeare)

4. It is not the post which colors the man, but the man the post.

5. A young man stopped by the store window.

6. "Young man" (a salutation).

7. "When this Peter grew up and often, to the benefit of his education and training, had to listen to remarks from the members of the troupe in which most often was repeated the word "man," he received the nickname of "man." The troupe consisted half of Germans, to whom, as also to other nations, the salutation "man" in quotation marks is used as a swear word, or at least as an insult." (Aage Madelung, *The Man From the Circus*)

8. "The Man from the Restaurant" (a title)

9. Man—the forehead of the age ("Chelovek—chelo veka").

Let us study these examples.

In the word "man" in all the examples (with the exception of the sixth and seventh), there is a general sign of meaning—the principal sign, but it quite noticeably varies in all by means of *its own* (secondary) signs of meaning.

In the first example, we have the syntactical isolation of the word "man" in the beginning of the phrase. This isolation aids in making the objective connection with other members of the clause also disappear; the idea of the meaning remains. Thus, in the given case, the quality of the isolating intonation acquires great importance as an emotional element which accompanies it. These secondary (in the given case, emotional) elements enter into the structure of "meaning."

Further on this coloring is maintained and modified: "Man—is you, I, he." This sentence gives the secondary sign an objective coloring. Here the peculiar intonation of the "open word-combination" (a term of Wundt's) is again important, significantly weakening this quality of an object. But this objective quality is immediately denied: "Man is not you, not I, not he." This sentence effaces the objective coloring.

67

Here is yet another example of semantic coloring in the presence of syntactical isolation (but occurring not in the beginning, but in the end of a grammatical unit), with analogous intonation:

> In high rank let him not forget
> The holiest of callings: man.

Meanwhile, in the example:

> Yes, he was a man, on the entire earth
> I will never find such a man,

is revealed the strength of the first complex of secondary signs, and the intensity of coloring which is communicated over a distance. If we take separately the phrase:

> On the entire earth
> I will never find such a man,

we will not have before us the secondary signs met in previous examples of "lofty" word-usage. (The phrase is near to a phrase such as: "such a man as he" or "such a man one will not find.") Here the secondary signs which are blended in are not at all like those which are present in phrases such as: "Man—it rings proudly" or "the holiest of callings: man."

Meanwhile, the phrase taken separately by us is preceeded by the following:

> "Yes, he was a man,"

where the word "man" is similar in terms of its secondary signs to the usage in the phrases: "Man—it rings proudly" and "the most holy of callings: man." And here, in the preceding phrase, the coloring is so strong and the syntactic connection between both clauses is so tight that it is even retained in the phrase following after it (that is, the one examined separately by us):

> Yes, he was a man,—on the entire earth
> I will never find such a man.

Let us now take the proverb:

> It is not the post which colors the man, but the man the post.

It is as though quite another word were before us. Although there is the preservation of the principal sign, there is nothing here which is

68

characteristic of the preceding examples of secondary signs.[56]

In the group "a young man stood by the store window," we have a curious oscillation of the principal sign and its partial obscuring. There is still the possibility here of retaining the principal sign completely, having restored the series "young man—old man," but closer to this word-usage is the salutation "young man," where both words are intimately connected and where the meaning of the attribute to a large degree effaced the principal sign of that which is being defined.[57] This allowed it to become a salutation to any *young* male. (This intimate connection is even expressed in the facultative deformation of the second member: "cheek.")

This meaning of the isolated group "young man" may so strongly color the non-isolated group "a young man stood by the store window," that in the word "man," upon its retaining of independence and even of its principal sign of meaning, there advances a *group coloring* in the capacity of a secondary sign. This may quite obscure the principal sign. This time, however, the secondary sign is not emotional.

The effacement of the principal sign of the word "man" in the group "young man" plays a group role, and is a negative secondary sign (since it is related to the entire group). But this effacement may sometimes allow other positive secondary signs to advance. This occurs in the characteristic salutation in a restaurant of the pre-revolutionary era: "Chelovek!" ("Waiter!").[58] Here secondary signs quite displace the principal one, occupy its place, and in turn acquire other emotional secondary signs. (Consider the fragment from Aage Madelung.)

Thus, in the isolation created by the title "The Man from the Restaurant," the word "man" may be a *play* of meanings. "Man" is connected here with two opposing series: man = "Man," where specific secondary signs advance, and man ("chelovek") = "cheek," where the place of the principal sign is occupied by secondary signs of a different, opposing character in comparison with "Man." Thus, in the title "The Man from the Restaurant," there is before us a word-usage in which the place of the principal sign is occupied at once by signs of two series, and this feature of mutual displacement unusually complicates the meaning.

Let us now examine the pun (of Andrei Bely): "Man—the forehead of the age" ("Chelovek—chelo veka").

What nuances advance in the meaning of the word "chelovek?" Thanks to the pun, there occurs a type of *redistribution of its material and formal parts*.[59] They become semasiological. It is clear that this feature of the parts becoming semasiological colors the word "chelovek" in a particular way. The coloring here is not obtained at the expense of the destruction of the principal sign (the destruction of the principal sign would entail the destruction of the pun, which consists precisely of the confrontation of two plans), but at the expense of its stability. Before us is a type of double semantics with two plans, each of which has particular principal signs, and

69

which mutually crowd each other. The oscillation of two semantic plans may lead to the partial obscuring of the principal sign, and advance oscillating signs of meaning. Here, in the given case, the lexical coloring of the words "chelo" and "vek" (their belonging, especially in the first case, to a "lofty" lexical system) plays a large role. Thus, this example shows that particularities of word-usage call forth secondary signs, which, in view of their instability, we may call *oscillating*.

But it also may occur that oscillating signs may quite displace the principal sign of meaning. The fact of the matter is that expressiveness of speech may be given by other means than the meanings of words. Words may be important even apart from their meanings, serving as vocal elements carrying another expressive function. For example, with a strong, emphatic intonation may be given a series of words indifferent in meaning, but which serve the auxiliary function of "filling in" the intonational series with verbal material. (Consider swearing intonations with their indifferent words.) Among the particular phenomena of this order is the strong, intonationally-emphatic coloring of auxiliary and secondary words, which quite obscures their principal sign of meaning. Instead of this principal sign, *oscillating* signs may advance.

In the given case the very *lexical* coloring of the word received un-usual importance *as a permanent secondary sign* of meaning. The clearer the lexical characteristic of the word, the greater the chances that upon obscuring the principal meaning, the lexical coloring of the word will advance into the light rather than its principal sign. Here usage of swear words in the capacity of endearment is extremely typical. These words carry the function of filling in the emphatic intonation with vocal material. Here the principal sign of the meaning of the words is effaced, and the *lexical coloring* remains as a connecting link, placing a given word in a particular series. The sense and strength of such a usage of a word, with a lexical coloring which opposes its intonational coloring, lies precisely in the sensation of this lack of con-vergence. Karl Schmidt observes that just as expensive perfume is not poured into a scented jar, so that one may smell the perfume, and not the jar, so are swear words chosen as endearments. A lexical element which is opposed to the emotional and intonational coloring compels it to advance all the more strongly.

2. Lexical Coloring

Thus, upon examination of the question of oscillating signs which appear in the word, the lexical coloration of the word acquires special im-portance. Upon the obscuring of the meaning (and, perhaps, of the principal sign of meaning), the general coloring of the word, which results from its belonging to a certain verbal environment, advances all the more clearly.

Every word is colored by the verbal environment in which it is chiefly used. The distinction of one verbal environment from another depends on the distinction of conditions and functions of linguistic activity. Each activity and state has its own particular conditions and goals, and, in dependence on these, either one or another word will receive a greater or lesser significance. The word will be drawn into these conditions.

The coloring of the word is all the more stronger when characteristic of the activity or environment which first altered and created it. Thus, *lexical coloring is realized only outside the activity and conditions for which it is characteristic.* In a strict sense, each word has its own lexical coloring (created by the epoch, nationality, and environment), but this *lexical distinctiveness* is recognized only outside this epoch and nationality. In this sense, lexical coloring serves as evidence. In a Berlin court, one word of *Gaunersprache* is sufficient, as is "thieves' music" with us, for the word to become evidence, *besides still bearing its principal sign of meaning, and even in spite of it.* (In the same way, foreign and dialectal coloring of speech has this character of evidence or shibboleth.)

Every verbal environment thus possesses an assimilative strength, which compels the word to carry particular functions, and colors them with the tone of its activity. The peculiarity and specificity of the functions of language in literature determines lexical selection. Every word is placed in and assimilated to them, but in order to be present in verse, the lexical coloring of the word must be realized constructively in the plan of literature:

> The traditional character of literature, (writes Paul,) colors the verbal material. The national epos of the Middle Ages, the courtly chivalric novel, the Minnesong, etc., leave unaffected an entire mass of words. The word enters into literature only under definite conditions.[60]

The reference to tradition is vital, but does not exhaust the matter. A poetic vocabulary is not only created by way of continuation of a particular lexical tradition, but also by the method of opposing itself to it (the vocabulary of Nekrasov and Mayakovsky). "Literary language" develops, and this development cannot be understood as a systematic development of tradition, but rather as colossal displacements of tradition (in which the partial restoration of older layers plays a large role).

A much more essential consideration is one introduced by Paul in another place:

> A well-developed style, one of whose laws is: do not repeat one and the same expression too often, naturally demands that one and the same thought have as many means of expression as possible. To an even greater degree, it demands possibilities of *choice* from several words with an identical meaning, words with definite sound structure,

71

meter, rhyme, and alliteration (for in the opposite case, their coercion (*Zwang*) might become unpleasant). Because of this, poetic language uses an equal-valued plurality of expressions created by chance. It in turn makes use of this plurality, where conversational language attaches the usage of each word to definite conditions. It retains this plurality where conversational language gradually moves toward unity. It is easy to demonstrate that the wealth of the poetic language of any people or epoch stands in an intimate connection with existing poetic techniques. It is easiest to do this with Old German alliterative poetry, which is distinguished by a special wealth of synonyms for the most ordinary concepts. The possibility of choice here serves the facilitation of alliteration."[61]

Words are not only selected, but are even created first. Wölfflin writes:

Metri causa, Lucretius and Virgil created forms which they introduced into the hexameter, such as 'maximitas' instead of 'magnitudo,' 'nominito' instead of 'nomino'... 'supvervacuus' instead of 'supervacaneus,' which was used in older prose, received diffusion via the poets using hexameter, namely, Horace and Ovid."[62]

From the point of view of stimulation of vocabulary by meter and other conditions of verse, those phenomena which are not immediately obvious are also interesting. For example, a linguistic fact such as the use of truncated adjectives by Pushkin was undoubtedly called for by either meter or the conditions of verse. Concerning the lines of Batyushkov: "Gde besprobudnym snom pechalny teni spiat" ("Where in deep slumber sad shadows sleep") (Tibullov elegy III, from book three), Pushkin noted: "The verses are remarkable in their fortunate truncation; we are too careful of truncation, which imparts much liveliness to verse."[63] (Perhaps Pushkin had in mind here the tight contiguity of the epithet and that which is defined.)

Thus, the engagement of a particular lexical stream into verse always must be realized constructively.

Lomonosov's use of Church Slavicisms and dialectisms was realized constructively.

Constructing the ode on the basis of the most emotional force, connecting words not by their principal sign, but rather so that secondary signs of meaning received particular importance, Lomonosov argued thus for Church Slavicisms:

In accordance with the importance of the sanctified place of God's church and antiquity, I feel in myself a somewhat special respect for the Slavic language (Old Church Slavic—trans.), with which the author especially ennobles splendid thoughts" ("On the Use of Church Slav-isisms").

Of course, the introduction of lexical elements of the Church Slavic lan-guage as a *language* is not important here, but rather as a language connected with a particular *activity* and its coloring. (Pushkin called Church Slavicisms "Biblicalisms.") Lomonosov also recognized the engagement of dialectisms from the point of view of their functional action (the comic).

It was not necessary to carry over an actual, real dialect in this matter, but was sufficient to aim toward a dialect or the coloring of a dialect, and a literary dialect, i.e., one necessary to literature, was found.[64]

But the literary vocabulary itself, in the capacity of tradition, in its turn is a lexically colored source for literature. Here the fate of several lexical phenomena is typical. The word "Nord" is a barbarism for Tred-yakovsky, Lomonosov, and perhaps, for Derzhavin and Petrov. But in the epoch of the mid-nineteenth century, the word "Nord," precisely because of its usage by older writers, became an archaism. Such was its role in Tyut-chev—an orientation toward archaic poets. The reverse current in the use of archaisms is interesting. Having become *traditional*, they became signs of *traditionality*, and the nineteenth century used them in the capacity of an "ironic vocabulary."[65] (Here, of course, the struggle of the Shishkov-ites and the Karamzinians played its own role, creating the *parodical* lit-erature of Arzamas, which became the literary source of parodical vocabu-lary.) Such was its role with the poet-archaists. Consider Tyutchev:

Pushek grom i musikiia!"

The thunder of cannon and music!

(with an ironic nuance). The lexical characteristic of the word is its con-stant secondary sign, which should not be confused with unstable, oscillating signs.

3. The Influence of Verse on the Sense of Words

The rhythmical verse series presents an entire system of conditions which distinctively influence the principal and secondary signs of meaning and the appearance of oscillating signs.

The first such factor is the *factor of the unity of the series*. Among the factors stimulating the sharpness and definiteness of this unity, one must take into account the relatively greater or lesser *independence* of the series. As is easily observed, short series, metrically monotonous, are much less independent and more connected with each other both rhythmically and syntactically than series which are relatively longer or metrically diverse. This obviously is connected with the concept that a part of a series, having received independence, is transformed, as it were, into a series. This limitation of the metrical independence of series calls forth an even weaker perception of their boundaries, which is necessary to take into account upon analysis.

Every verse series isolates and intensifies its own boundaries. More weakly isolated, but nevertheless isolated, are the internal divisions of the series—the boundaries of periods, etc.

We may observe how strong the feature of division in verse is in the following instance:

1. *Kogda zari rumianyi polusvet*
2. *V okno tiur'my proshchal'nyi privet*
3. *Mne, umiraia, posylaet,*
4. *I opershis' na zvuchnoe ruzh'e,*
5. *Nash chasovoi, pro staroe zhit'e*
6. *Mechtaia, stoia zasypaet...*

1. When the ruddy twilight of dawn
2. Into the window of the prison its farewell greeting
3. To me, dying, sends,
4. And leaning upon his resounding gun,
5. Our guard, about the old life
6. Dreaming, stands dropping off to sleep...

Here the strength of the division in the penultimate (fifth) line is magnified by the stanzaic character of the poem. The fourth line, constructed quite the same metrically and rhymed with the fifth, adds weight to the abruptness of the division. The abruptness of the division is so great that we almost sever the line from the last one, which is syntactically connected with it.(The formal homogeneity of similar words in the sixth line ("mechtaia," "stoia") ("dreaming," "standing") also promotes this consciousness of the division, since they are difficult to separate.) However that may be, the condition of division is a compulsory fact of verse. I have already spoken about how non-observance of this fact results in the destruction of verse. Let us have yet one more example of the strength of verse unity from Batiushkov:

I gordyi um ne pobedit
Liubvi, kholodnymi slovami.

And the proud intellect will not conquer
Love, with cold words.

In the margins of his copy, Pushkin wrote: "The sense comes out as

74

such: *with cold words of love*; the comma does not help."[66]

(Here, as is easily observed, is revealed even a second factor: the *compact* connections of words in one series.)

Here is an example from Tyutchev:

Kak bednyi nishchii, mimo sadu
Bredet po zharkoi mostovoi.

Like a poor beggar, past the garden
He wanders along the hot roadway.

Even such an experienced elocutionist of verse as S. Volkonsky was inclined to consider the article of comparison not "a poor beggar," but "a poor beggar past the garden," that is, not: "like a poor beggar—he wanders past the garden," but: "like a poor beggar past the garden—he wanders... along the roadway."

An example from Lermontov's verse indicates the strength of the boundaries of periods:

No ne s toboi/ia serdtsem govoriu.

But not with you/will I speak sincerely.

The abrupt caesura here called forth (in connection with intonational consequences) a secondary signification:

No ne s toboi,/ ia s serdtsem govoriu.

But not with you,/ —I speak with my heart.

(So it was in the text of Lermontov printed in *Notes of the Fatherland*, 1843, volume 28.)

Each emphasis of these boundaries is a strong semantic means for *isolating* words. Such emphasis is usually a result of: 1. the importance of the boundary of a series (for example, in the tripartite division of the anapestic meter of the ballad, where the end of each series is simultaneously the end of the second period, amplified by its connection (via rhyme) with the end of the first period), 2. or a failure of these boundaries (of the series and the period) to converge with the boundaries of syntactical unity, that is, enjambment and interior *rejets*.

We will begin with the latter. The failure of the rhythmical series and syntactical unity to converge is reflected in a special intonational figure (an insufficient falling in the beginning of the second series, in connection with a pause). Understandably, these features may coincide with features which are semantically ordinary, so that they indicate and deepen particular nuances in the combination of members of the clause. This demonstrates a type of enjambment:

> *Vse khorosho, moi drug, no to li/*
> *Moia krasavitsa? Ona/*
> *Zavoevatel'nitsa voli*
> *I dlia poeta rozhdena.*

> All is fine, my friend, but as for/
> My beautiful one? She/
> Is a conqueror of the will
> And was born for the poet.   (Yazykov)

There is no doubt of the presence of enjambment here, but it emphasizes the interrogative complex "to-li" ("as for") in the first line, on which there is the ascending intonation of a question anyway. But on the word ending the enjambment, "krasavitsa" ("beauty"), on which there is a descending intonation, there is a rise in the beginning owing to the strength of the conclusion of the interrogative clause. In the second series it separates the word "ona" ("she") from the predicate, that is, there occurs an ordinary isolation of the subject.

Isolation of the subject is defined and emphasized in the following enjambment:

> *Prokhladen vozdukh byl; v stekle spokoinykh vod*
> *Zvezdami ubrannyi lazurnyi neba svod/*
> *Svetilsia;*
> *Vliublennyi iunosha i deva molodaia/*
> *Brodili vdol' reki...*
> *Dlia nikh tumanami okrestnaia dolina/*
> *Skryvalas'...*   (Yazykov, "Vecher")

> The air was fresh; in the glass of peaceful waters
> With stars the decorated azure heavenly vault/
> Shone;
> A young man in love and a young girl/
> Wandered along the river...
> For them by mists the neighboring valley/
> Was hidden...   ("Evening")

Here is enjambment emphasizing the isolation and intonation of a verbal adverb complex:

76

Liubliu ego, emu vnimaia,/
Ia naslazhdaius'...   *(Yazykov, "Ruchei")*

I love him, to him harking,/
I am delighted...   ("The Brook")

It is easiest of all to trace the semantic role of enjambment not where it emphasizes the syntactic pause and intonational line, but where it is *unmotivated*. It is easiest to observe this role in verses with a prosaic construction of phrases, in which the isolating role of enjambment is not, as it were, taken into consideration by the poet. Let us take an example from Polonsky:

Kura shumit, tolkaias'v temnyi/
Obryv skaly zhivoi volnoi...

The blizzard roars, rushing into the dark/
Precipice of rock with a living wave...

Here the isolation of the epithet "dark" from the defined "precipice of rock" is not motivated syntactically. [67] We almost can imagine that this is a prosaic phrase before us (as if from a story of Chekhov):

Kura shumit, tolkaias'v temnyi obryv skaly.

The blizzard roars, rushing into the dark precipice of rock.

Then the group "dark precipice of rock" is presented *simultaneously*. With a narrative intonation, the defined "precipice of rock" (and in this group, the last word "rock") receives greater strength, being defined and *colored* by the epithet "dark." With the simultaneity of this group, the epithet receives a more or less distinct object-like characteristic. It is reflected as an object-like sign of that which is defined. Meanwhile, in verse, ending the rhythmical series and being separated from the second rhythmical series, the epithet is suspended in air, as it were. Its reunification with that which is defined, found in the second rhythmical series, occurs with such a sensation of sequentialness that the epithet, being separated from its carrier, does not fulfill the function of object-like coloring. Instead of this, the principal sign of the word "dark" advances with particular strength, as do secondary, emotional signs. In view of the compactness of the rhythmical series, oscillating signs of meaning may even arise in the word, in intimate connection with the words of a given series. Thus, the word "temnyi" ("dark") may enter into a connection, called forth by sound, with the word "shumit" ("roars").

The seclusion of the series and the special semantic meaning of divisions is distinctly obvious in the example from the following poem:

Gliadi: eshchetsela za nami/
Ta saklia, gde tomu nazad/
Polveka, zhadnymi glazami/
Lovil ia serdtsu milyi vzgliad.

Look: still intact behind us/
That saklia,† where back/
A half-century, with greedy eyes/
I caught in my heart that loving glance.

(†"saklia" is a type of dwelling of Caucasian peoples.)

It is not difficult to note that the syntax here (and the vocabulary)
is deliberately oriented toward the prosaic, as if not concerned with divisions.
(In actual fact, the principal particularity of the poem consists of the emphasizing of divisions.[68])

We will attempt to write the stanza linearly, and, having forgotten for
the moment about verse, present it in the following manner:

Gliadi: eshche tsela za nami ta saklia, gde tomu nazad polveka
zhadnymi glazami lovil ia milyi vzgliad.

Look: still intact behind us that saklia, where back a half-century,
with greedy eyes I caught that loving glance.

(I have allowed myself to throw out one word from the last line which
deforms this line, and even further destroys verse associations.)

It is easy to note in these prosaic lines the words which bear a greater
syntactico-semantic weight. They are the major members of the clause,
as well as members which complete grammatical unities. Here are the strongest intonational points:

Gliadi: ta saklia: polveka: lovil ia: vzgliad.

Look: that saklia: half-century: I caught: glance.

Let us take them in verse.
1. The first rhythmical series is:

Gliadi: esche tsela za nami.

Look: still intact behind us.

78

The syntactical unity is not closed, which is revealed in the special rise in inclination of the first rhythmical series toward the second, but this rise does not at all destroy the unity and compactness of the rhythmical series. The reunion of the group: "eshche tsela za nami ta saklia" ("still intact behind us that saklia") occurs successively and consistently, "za nami" ("behind us"), with which the rhythmical series ends, being brought forward. The secondary role of these words does not correspond to their advanced position, and they are recognized as an isolated member. The words are suspended in air and isolated. The words "za nami" ("behind us") strongly reinforce the *spatial* meaning in the given case, which upon reunification with the following series, pass on the nuance "in relationship to him." Thus, the severance of the intonational line, defined by verse, results in occasional *distinctions of meanings of words in verse, as compared with their prosaic doubles.*

2. The second rhythmical series:

Ta saklia, gde tomu nazad

That saklia, where back

brings forward the semantic complex "tomu nazad" ("back," "ago"). In connection with the nuance of spatiality which is advanced in the first series, the temporal meaning of the word "nazad" ("back") pales somewhat, advancing the principal sign of the word. Thus, instead of the temporal meaning of the complex, a partially spatial nuance advances. In view of the determination of the spatial nuance by the word "tomu" (first member of the phrase "tomu nazad"-trans.), it will understandably be unstable and oscillating.

The law of semantic advancement of the end of the series may sometimes be used for the enlivening of an effaced metaphor. The liveliness of a metaphor is directly connected with the presence of the principal sign, emphasized, as we saw, in the end of a series.

Let us take the prosaic line:

Gor ne vidat'—vsia dal' odeta lilovoi mgloi.

The mountains cannot be seen—the entire distance dressed in a violet haze.

In the second clause, the word "odeta" ("dressed") is perceived quite palely relative to its principal sign. It has undergone a most complex evolution. From the first, one could clearly recognize the semantic heterogeneity of this word. The circumstance that such words as "dal'"("distance") and "gora" ("mountain") are connected with it, as though with a predicate, called forth in the word "odeta" ("dressed"): 1. a partial displacement of the principal sign, and 2. a partial presence of the meaning of words usually associated with the words "gora" ("mountain") and "dal'" ("distance"), in the given case, in the capacity of predicates. Its principal sign is effaced (for example, "covered"). But this, understandably, entered into the composition of meaning mostly in a negative way, in view of the connections displacing the principal sign of the word "odeta" ("dressed"). This shift of the principal sign always creates a semantic tension. But this semantic tension arises only as a result of a *partial* displacement of the principal sign. In order for a metaphor to be recognized as living, it demands that the *principal sign* in the word be sensed, but precisely in its narrowed, shifted aspect. As soon as the feature of this displacement is absent, as soon as the "struggle" is ended, metaphor dies. It becomes current and lingual.

This occurs by connections with other members of the metaphor (in the given case, with the subject) becoming solid and habitual, completely displacing the principal sign of meaning of one series.

In the line we are investigating, the metaphor is rather paled. This paling occurred for three reasons. The first is the habitualness of the connection. The second is owing to the character of the verbal form of a participle, which effaces to a certain degree the sign of the verb as an action, and pushes forward signs of constancy. Thirdly, the object enters into an intimate (because habitual) combination with the metaphor. The principal sign of the object, being quite weighty, displaces still further the principal sign of the verbal methaphor. The phrase "vsia dal' odeta lilovoi mgloi" ("the entire distance dressed in a violet haze") is usually distributed as follows (owing to the effacement which occurs for the indicated reasons):

vsia dal' odeta/lilovoi mgloi.

the entire distance/dressed in a violet haze.

The word "odeta" ("dressed") appears in the role of a member of the predicate. (We could just as well have said "covered," "shrouded," etc.) A special intonation is demanded in order to cancel the habitual combination "odeta mgloi" ("dressed in a haze"), and to emphasize the combination "dal' odeta" ("the distance is dressed"), so that the phrase takes on this shape:

vsia dal' odeta/lilovoi mgloi.

the entire distance dressed/in a violet haze.

In verse, owing to the unity of the verse series, the connection between the subject and predicate is renewed, but the object, carried to the next series, is reunited with the principal members of the clause only consecutively:

80

Gor ne vidat'—vsia dal' odeta/
Lilovoi mgloi...

The mountains cannot be seen—the entire distance dressed/
In a violet haze...

As a result, we have the *enlivening of the metaphor, conditioned by
the unity of the verse series.*

The unity of the series is revealed not only in the isolation of words
and groups, but in the even *greater significance of divisions.* Thus, if the
line is restricted to one word, so that firstly, we have the circumstance of
the word = the detached line, and secondly, it is built upon divison, this significantly increases the force of the word and isolates it. This in turn
promotes the enlivening of principal signs.

Consider Mayakovsky's "Heaven" ("Nebo")[69] :

Ogliadyvaius',
Eta vot
Zalizannaia glad',
Eto i est' khvalenoe nebo?
Posmotrim, posmotrim,
Iskrilo,
Sverkalo,
Blestelo
I
Shorokh shel
Oblako
Ili
Bestelye
Tikho skol'zili.

I look around,
This here
Licked clean smoothness,
Is this the much-praised heaven?
Let us look, let us look.
It sparkled,
It glittered,
It shone
And
A rustle went
A cloud
Or
Spirits
Quietly glided.

81

One should pay special attention to the auxiliary words and particles: "i" ("and") and "ili" ("or"), which, being advanced, add quite a new aspect to the construction of the clause. The more insignificant and unobtrusive the advanced word, the more its advancement deforms speech (and sometimes even animates the principals signs in these words).

This advancement by means of division (in connection with rhyme) of auxiliary words is one of the devices of Pushkin in *Eugene Onegin*. Also consider Lermontov:

> *Vsegda kipit i zreet chto-nibud'/*
> *V moie grudi...*

There always seethes and ripens something/
In my breast...

The group "chto-nibud'" ("something") has a group sense, a *groupe articulée* according to the terminology of Breal[76], so that neither the first or second (or third) of its members is conceived of separately. Of the two members of the group, the major one is that on which the stress lies. In the given case, in a normal prosaic construction this would be:

> *vsegda kipit i zreet chto-nibud' v moie grudi.*

"there always seethes and ripens something in my breast."

The second word ("nibud'"—trans.) is reduced for accentual reasons. In verse, division advances the third member "bud'" with great strength, since this is where the metrical stress lies. Thus, instead of the group "chto' nibud'," we have "chto' nibud'," This significantly sets off the word,"rehabilitating it." This action of divisions on speech, which arises as a result of making verse vocabulary and genres prosaic (*Eugene Onegin*) is typical. That which appears in conversation and prosaic speech as only a necessary auxiliary property is elevated here to the *level of full equality with words,* advancing by means of division.

That which is clear in the example of one-word series is not so clear in other examples (since the principle of operation of the series as one word falls away here). Nevertheless, one may observe the action of *divisions* on ordinary verses and inside ordinary verses. Let us consider the following example.

In language, there are words which replace other groups of words with themselves, in which they appear as significant members (usually as a member more strongly modulated in a group[71]). Such substitution, arising on the basis of the intimate connections of one word with others, may lead to a complete loss of the word's principal sign of meaning. At that time, the word, losing this principal sign, acquires the meaning of the group. Rosenstein calls this "associative substitution of meaning" (*Assoziativer Bedeutungswechsel*), while Wundt calls it "condensation of a concept through syntactical association" (*Begrifsverdichtung durch syntaktishe Assoziation*). Bréal and Darmesteter call it "infection" ("contagion"). Here words in a group act on each other, as though infecting one another with their proximity, because of which one word may represent the entire group.[72]

Without a doubt, this is a protracted process. At its beginning, we have the usage of a member of a group for the meaning of the entire group, but with a partial preservation of the principal sign of the proper meaning. Before us is the phrase: "Baron poblednel i zasverkal na nego glazami" ("The baron paled and glared at him with his eyes"). The group "zasverkal glazami" ("glared with his eyes") may be expressed with only one verb: "zasverkal" ("glared"): "Baron poblednel i zasverkal na nego" ("The baron paled and glared at him"). Although one cannot speak of the substitution of meaning here, there is "associative condensation," and it is at the expense of a partial paling of the principal sign in the meaning of the verb "sverkat'" ("to glare"). Now let us consider a phrase such as "Baron vskipel" ("The baron flew into a rage") or "Baron kipel" ("The baron seethed"), or even "Baron kipel i gorel" ("The baron seethed and burned"). The principal sign in the meaning will be almost as pale as in the phrase "Baron rval i metal" ("The baron ranted and raved").

If we say "Baron i kipel, i gorel, i sverkal" ("The baron seethed, and burned, and glared"), the principal signs of the verbs are hardly intensified. We have an intonation created by the repeated connecting conjunction "i" ("and"), with which the principal signs of the homogeneous members pale. (The intonational line has a monotonal character. This creates a nuance of *potential* repetition, as if not restricted by the given members, which emphasizes their *homogeneity*. This in turn pales the individual principal signs in the meanings of the homogeneous members.)

Consider the lines of Zhukovsky:

> *I Smal'gol'mskii baron, porazhen, razdrazhen,*
> *I kipel, i gorel, i sverkal.*

> And baron Smalgolmsky, defeated, angry,
> Seethed, and burned, and glared.

Before us is the tripartite line of the ballad. The second part in turn breaks up into two members, and the third part into three members. The divisions inside the line are:

> *I kipel   i gorel   i sverkal*

Seethed   and burned   and glared.

These divisions are connected with some definite verse intonation, with which the nuance of potential repetition disappears.

Thus, since the reunion of the members of the clause here takes place because of a successive metrical articulation, and each member of the clause has the significance of a rhythmical member, there occurs an *intensifying of the principal sign*, which progressively increases. The intensifying of the principal sign in the first member of the clause creates conditions more favorable for its intensification in following members. The last word, located simultaneously on the divisions of the period and the series, intensifies it even more, and, to a certain degree, colors it a second time upon the closing of the group. Thus, there occurs something on the order of the *realization of a linguistic stamp*, which in the given case adds a light, *comical coloring*.

In the same way, one may observe even the action of a caesura, not quite as abrupt, but nonetheless real, in the breakup of such groups into epithet and that which is defined, etc.

4. Rhythmical Significance and Semantic Significance

In several of the last examples, the action of the unity of the verse series has joined with the action of a more complex factor—the isolation of words in accord with their *greater rhythmical significance*. This fact, as I have already indicated, is dependent to a certain degree on the dynamics of the vocal material.

Even the attention of ancient theoreticians dwelled upon semantic emphasis and isolation of certain words by means of rhythm. At the basis of Longinus' study on the "order of words" lay the study of "harmony," in which it is not difficult to distinguish a position on the emotional nuances of meaning which are dependent on rhythm (section 39):

Harmony not only naturally produces in man conviction and pleasure, but even serves as an amazing tool for the elevation of the soul and passion. For the pipe arouses in listeners several passions, and as though depriving one of one's mind, it brings about madness. Having placed in our souls the trace of meter, it compels us to move according to that meter... After this, we can hardly doubt that the *composition of words, this harmony of the word* innate to man, strikes not only the hearing, but even the very soul. It arouses in us various images, names, thoughts, things, beauties, and melodies, having some connection and affinity with our soul. Together with the mixture and diversity of its sounds, it pours into the listeners the passions of the orator, making them into participants. With the *composition of words*

84

this harmony of the word innate to man, strikes not only the hearing, but even the very soul. It arouses in us various images, names, thoughts, things, beauties, and melodies, having some connection and affinity with our soul. Together with the mixture and diversity of its sounds, it pours into the listeners the passions of the orator, making them into participants. With the *composition of words accompanied by greatness of thought*, we can hardly doubt that it is by means of this that our souls are quite won over. Now we are pleased, now we are instilled with a certain pride, majesty, and elevation, and all the beauties found in these... Thus, the thought articulated by Demosthenes is quite great... But the harmony does not yield to the beauty of the thought, for every measure consists of dactylic feet... If only one word is shifted from its place to another... or one iota is severed... then it is easy to perceive how harmony promotes the *lofty*. For these words (concluding–Yu. T.) "like a cloud," leaning upon the first long foot, are measured in four ways, so that if one iota is taken away: "like a cloud," then, with such a severance, the loftiness disappears. And on the contrary, if one were to extend the above... even though the meaning of the words were the same, the incidence is not the same. The precipitous loftiness is destroyed and weakened by the length of these last bits."[73]

Here we note the curious definition of the assimilative strength of meter: "having placed in our souls the trace of meter, it compels us to move according to that meter"; "verbal harmony strikes not only the hearing, but the soul itself"; "attending 'composition' and 'harmony' is 'greatness of thought'."

Boileau perceived the formula: "L'harmonie ne frappe pas seulement l'oreille, mail l'esprit" ("Harmony touches not only the ear, but the spirit also"), but then narrowed it to an unrecognizable state:

> *Le vers le mieux rempli, la plus noble pensée*
> *Ne peut plaire à l'esprit quan l'oreille est blessée.*

> The best completed verse, the most noble thought
> Is not able to please the spirit when the ear is offended.

The concept of "interaction" and "harmony of words" receded into the background before the concept of "correspondence" and "motivation of rhythm." Consider Marmontel's comments on Fléchier.

The concept of "harmony" was perceived by the translator of Longinus, Martynov, through the prism of Boileau. He significantly narrowed and distorted it in his notes, having equated "harmony" with oratorical rhythm. It is curious that Batyushkov, who was studying Longinus, revived the concept of "harmony" in his complex manner. Making a copy of Lomonosov, he emphasizes several words in the verses:

Inoi ot sil'nogo udara ubegaia,
Stremglav na niz sletel i stonet *pod konem;*
Inoi pronzen ugas, *protivnika pronzaia;*
Inoi vraga poverg i umer *sam na nem...*

One from a strong blow running away,
Headlong down he fell and *groans* beneath the horse;
Another having been pierced is *perishing,* piercing his enemy;
Another threw down the enemy and *died* himself upon him...

He then adds: "We note in passing what strength the most ordinary words receive for the poet when they are provided with their proper place" ("Ariost i Tass").

This was apparently one of the major points of the work of Batyushkov on poetic language. Besides in the area of vocabulary and euphony, contemporaries recognized the peculiarity of his language precisely in the subtle *semantic utilitization of the interaction of rhythm and syntax.*

Thus, the full extent of the concept of "harmony" was revived. In 1822, Pletnev wrote about Batyushkov and Zhukovsky:

Purity, freedom and *harmony* constitute the major perfections of our verse language... Above all it is necessary to distinguish *harmony from melody.* The latter is easily attained first: it is based on consonance of sounds. Where their selection is successful, the hearing is not outraged, and there is no difficulty in articulation, there we have melody. It has an even higher degree, when the merger of sounds definitely expresses some type of phenomenon in nature, and, like music, imitates it. Harmony demands *completeness of sounds, depending on the comprehension of thoughts* or definite approximations (as does a statue), in accordance with their value. A small, meager face, even if the features are pleasant, always seems wrong with a large trunk. *Each feeling, each thought of the poet has its own comprehension.* Taste is not able to mathematically define it, but it senses when it finds it in verses, whether it be decreased or exaggerated, and says: this is not complete, while this is prolix. These subtelties of verse may be observed only by poets. One must place Zhukovsky and Batyushkov in the first rank.[74]

This "comprehension" is without a doubt a designation for the action of rhythm on semantics. This results in an *alteration of the semantic significance of the word, which receives as a result a rhythmical significance.*

86

The most simple example of such an impact is the isolation of the word in the so-called "pauznik." (I spoke above on how speech is made dynamic in the "pauznik.") Here it is as if there were a surplus of metrical energy, concentrated on a particular word or on several words. This emphasizes and isolates the word to a certain degree:

Zdes' lezhala ego treugolka
I rastrepannyi tom *Parni.*

Here lay his cocked hat
And tattered *volume* of Parny.

The word "tom" ("volume") proves to be the most dynamic here, but even the following word proves to be isolated.

We also see this in the lines:

I skazala: gospodi bozhe,
Primi raba tvoego.

And she said: lord god,
Take your servant.

In the word "skazala" ("she said") in the first line, there is a surplus of metrical energy, and the word proves to be dynamic and isolated; but this is also imparted to the following word. The same thing applies in the second line. Since the last words, however, are isolated and emphasized by their very position, standing on the boundary of the series, it happens that the "pauznik" *operates with isolated words*, and the entire phrase receives a successive character. In the above example, such isolation of words is motivated by their emotional lexical sign.

But, for example, in the lines:

Na shelkovom *odeiale*
Sukhaia lezhala ruka...

On the *silk* blanket
Dry lay a hand...

this dynamism and isolation of words is not motivated, so that there is a successive reunion of the epithet with what is defined. This promotes the enlivening of the principal sign of the word in the epithet before the reunion, coloring the entire group. It is curious that even the second line: "Sukhaia lezhala ruka" ("Dry lay a hand"), with its properly impeccable "amphibrachic trimeter," is subordinated to the metrical and semantic construction of the whole. It also is perceived as a "pauznik" with isolated words. The way in which speech is made *dynamic* in verse is thus revealed

87

in the area of semantics by the isolation of words, and by the elevation of the semantic feature in them. This results in all of the consequences of the semantics of detached words and of their general successive movement.

The conditions of such an isolation are many. One must note, however, that such an isolation is only a partial incident of the general phenomenon of the *semantic significance* of the word in verse being defined *by the significance of rhythm. The word in verse is always made dynamic, and is always advanced, but vocal processes are successive.* This is why a stanza of four lines, or two lines, or even of one line (consider Karamzin and Briusov) may be a legitimate form of poetry, whereas in prose, the form of the aphorism is sensed as *fragmentary.* But on the contrary, the quantity of words in a series, the magnitude of the series, its independence (lines which are quite short and monotonous in meter are less independent), and, finally, the character of the meter and character of the stanza are not indifferent for the semantic structure.

(In the latter case, two basic types of stanzas are important: 1. that which may be called a closed metrical unity, of the type $a+b$, $a+n+n+b$, $a+n+b+n$, etc., with a constant quantity of series; and 2. that which may be called an open unit : $a+n+n^1+n^2+...+b$, $a+n+n^1+b+n+n^1+n^2...$ In the second type, the quantity of intervening series is inconsistent and vascillating, and bears the character of a "filling-up" of the unit.)

Indicating the action of *divisions*, I unintentionally touched upon an example revealing the greatest strength of divisions. This case (Mayakovsky) was coupled with the case of the line equalling one word. If we remember that with *vers libre* the lines are sharply distinguished by the quantity of words, and that *vers libre* presents an "altered metrical" system, it becomes clear that *it is also an "altered" system semantically.* Advancing some words, moving and bringing together others, it redistributes the semantic weight of the clause.

"Comprehension" of every word creates unusual results with auxiliary words, which acquire an eminent place in verse according to their duration:

I v pelenakh ostavila svirel',
Kotoruiu *sama zavorozhila.*

And in the shrouds she left a pipe,
Which she herself cast a spell over.

Here the word "kotoruiu" ("which") is made so dynamic that it no longer corresponds to its modest purpose and lacklustre sign of meaning. Being made dynamic, it is filled with *oscillating signs* which now come forward.

In his time, A. S. Shishkov, one of the most remarkable of Russian semasiologists, observed the dynamics of the word in verse and the *amplification* of its meaning.[75]

He made the following remark on the composition of a Sumarokov fable:

Tolchki proezzhü chuet
I v nos, i v rylo, i v boka,
Odnako, epancha gorazdo zhestoka:
Khlopochet,
I s nim idti ne khochet.

Bumps the traveller feels
In the nose, and the mug, and the side,
However, the epancha† is quite cruel:
It bangs,
And with him does not wish to go.

(†epancha is a broad cloak.)

In such verses as written parables, fables, and tales, which demand a simple, free, and amusing style, identically measured lines are not as proper for play and jokes as are lines of diverse measure, that is, long mixed with short, often consisting of one word. For example, the verb "khlopochet" ("it bangs"), *taking the place of an entire line, could not possibly have the same amount of strength if it were together with other words, rather than standing so unusually alone.* This is good for two reasons. First, in standing alone, it indicates its own strength better, and, second, it unites in itself two concepts. For "khlopochet," speaking about a human, means *to fuss, to worry.* Speaking about lifeless things, it means *to be continually banging* or *to tremble.* This latter signification we feel since the verbs "topaet" ("stamp") and "khlopaet" ("flap") are frequent, otherwise we could not say "topochet" ("clatter") and "khlopochet" ("bang"). The epancha represents two things at once here. In one case, the verb "khlopochet" is exactly like "ne khochet" ("does not want"), depicting something exceptional with the feelings of a creature. In the second case, the verb "khlopochet" depicts the epancha as a thing without feelings, trembling in the wind. *This combination of concepts in one and the same word creates beauty of representation. For many thoughts are born in the mind as short dicta."*[6]

Here the dynamics of the word in verse is quite well depicted, as well as the emphasizing of the collision of principal signs which is a result of this.

The fable, which in the second half of the nineteenth century was given to children in school, was the comic genre in the eighteenth century and first decades of the nineteenth century. It was perceived and judged from the point of view of "the beauties *of verse.*" These "beauties" were in the original *vers libre* of the fable, the basis of which was the sharp variability of the quantity of words in a line. In connection with the inequality of words as members of a clause, and with the intentional "common peopleness" (the literary "vulgarity" of the vocabulary) which was appointed to the fable, this peculiarity gave a comical coloring to the genre. Uneven semantic shading and coloring, accomplished on special material, advanced its originality with great force, disturbing the ordinary proportions of classical verse (even of the classical "vers libre" epoch). From this we obtain the kinship of the fable with the comedy in verse.

This weight of words has an influence on the transformation of poetic language. In various epochs it is the means of their selection. In 1871 Count A. K. Tolstoy wrote to Ia. P. Polonsky:

> I began to write a drama on Novgorod. I wrote three acts right off in Dresden, in prose... But the other day I glanced at the manuscript, and with grief began to set the prose into verses, and what a miracle! Immediately all was cleansed, all that was useless fell away of itself, and it became clear to me that it is easier for me to write verses than prose! *Here all types of chatter so clearly advance that you rush to cross it out.*[77]

5. Oscillating Signs of Meaning in Verse

Kireevsky wrote even much earlier on the semantic significance of the word depending on its significance in verse. There are other features here as well, however:

> Do you know why you have not written anything as yet? Because you do not write verses. If only you wrote verses, you would then love to express *even idle thoughts, and every word, well-said, would have for you the value of great thoughts.* And this is necessary for the writer with a soul. Then you would only write when it is enjoyable to write. But for whomever to elegantly express something does not have a *distinctive charm, separate from the object,* it is not pleasant to write. And so, do you wish to be a good writer in prose? Then write verses."[77a]

Thus, not only do "all types of chatter so clearly advance that you rush to cross it out," but it is not even necessary to cross it out. In verse, it is enjoyable to express idle thoughts, in which *each* word well-said acquires the significance and value of great thoughts.

Here, of course, we have not only the dynamization of words and their isolation (for then it would do "to cross out the chatter," and one would not have the "value of great thoughts"). There is also a type of "charm, separate from the object."

Let us also remember the words of Goethe:

> "Speaking of the works of our newest poets, we came to the

90

conclusion," wrote Eckermann, "that not one of them is able to write good prose. 'The matter is simple.' said Goethe. *'In order to write prose, one must have something to say*, but someone who has nothing to say may still write verses and select rhymes, in which one word prompts another, and *something at last will come out. And although it also does not mean anything, it seems as if it means something!*'"[78]

We will forget the mocking tone of Goethe (or is it Eckermann?). Let us consider his definition of the "new lyric poetry"—to say nothing, that is, to *communicate* nothing. Thoughts, which are required in an objectification, are absent. Here the process of creation does not strive for communicative goals. (Meanwhile prose, with its simultaneous arrangement, is communicative to a much greater degree: "In order to write prose, one must have something to say.")

The very process of creation is depicted by Goethe as completely successive: "one word prompts another." (Here Goethe allots a large role to rhymes.) "And although it also does not mean anything, it seems as if it means something." Here is the point at which Goethe collides with Kireevsky ("the well-said word has the value of great thoughts"). Thus, both are concerned with *"empty" words in the broad sense of the term, which receive a type of "apparent semantics" in verse.*

That which Goethe (or Eckermann) ridicules, Novalis defends: "One can imagine to oneself stories without connections, but in association, like dreams—poems, full of beautiful words, but without any sense or connection. Only some stanzas will be understood, like heterogeneous fragments." (Here, incidentally, it is important to note the demand for "beautiful words.")

One of the earliest investigators of semantics, Alfred Rosenstein, attempted to scientifically substantiate this concept of "empty words" (*Die psychologische Bedingungen des Bedeutungswechsels der Wörter*, Danzig, 1884). He attempted to do this by maintaining that the specificity of verse lay in the semantic relationship, proceeding from the role of verse as an emotional system. The basic position which allowed him to make these conclusions was the "meaning of the word is defined by the totality of connections (*Gesamtheit*) of not only the concepts, but also of the emotions":

I conclude from this psychological fact, that the large portion of impact rendered on us by the lyrical and lyrico-epic poet. When we are disposed (or should be disposed) so that we expect the movement of our feelings, the corresponding notions of words are less aroused in us than the emotions connected with them. There immediately rises a certain mood in us when the poet says:

Wer Reitet so spat durch *Nacht* und Wind?
Who rides so late through *night* and wind?

But in the following line, other emotional tones begin to ring-

> Es ist der *Vater* mit seinem Kind!
>
> It is the *father* with his child!

This answer, which in relation to the area of our notions, is quite empty, may be unusually interesting for our feelings."[79]

The concept of artistic emotion is based here somewhat rashly on the fact that the question and answer is "rhetorical" and "empty." (But even the "emptiness" here is not typical. It is "empty" in the example quoted, of course, from the point of view of everyday communication. Practically speaking, many chapters of novels, with their familiar "strangers," are like this also. In the plan of construction before us is the phenomenon which may be called the "unwinding of the lyrical plot" (the terminology of V. Shklovsky), occurring by means of the particular image inherent to it. Meanwhile, Novalis speaks about the absence of "sense and connection" inside the construction.) But the very concept of "artistic emotion" proves to be precarious.

The concept of "artistic emotion" is characterized in quite some detail by Wundt:

> Emotions, directly associated with the (aesthetic) objects themselves, are shaped in their own specific properties by the same correlation which stands between the parts of the given presentation. Since this correlation is something objective, independent of the particular method of influence on us, then it significantly promotes the pushing aside of general subjective feelings which are peculiar to aesthetic impressions.[79a]

Thus, the concept of "artistic emotion" displays its hybrid nature, and returns above all to the question of the objective "correlation of parts of the presentation" which defines it. That is, it returns to the question of the construction of the artistic work. (The pushing aside of general "subjective feelings" is, incidentally, a sufficient refutation of the naively-psychological approach to poetic semantics from the point of view of mere emotional associations connected with words.)

And so, one should replace the all-to-general reference of Rosenstein to the emotional nature of verbal presentations in verse with the position on the "objective correlation of parts of the presentation," *as defined by the construction of the artistic work*. Together with the secondary role of general subjective feelings falls out the vulgar concept of "mood." The order and character of presentations of meaning depend, of course, not on mood, but on the order and character of vocal activity.

And so, according to what was said above, there remain two theses: 1. there is a partial absence of "content" in verbal presentations in verse ("inhaltlos"); and, 2. the word in verse bears a particular semantic value according to its position. Words prove to be in stronger and nearer correlations and connections inside verse series and unities than in ordinary speech. This strength of connection does not leave the character of the semantics untouched.

In a given series (in verse), the word may be quite "empty," that is, 1. the principal sign of its meaning may introduce an extremely small new element, or 2. it may even be not quite connected with the general "sense" of the rhythmico-syntactic unity. Meanwhile, the action of the *compactness* of the series reaches even to it: "although nothing is said, it seems as if something is said." The fact of the matter is that *oscillating signs* of meaning may advance, defined by the compactness of the series (by the compact proximity). These may be intensified at the expense of the principal sign and in place of it, creating a "semblance of meaning" or an "apparent meaning."

Polevoy wonderfully described the origin of oscillating signs of meaning in the presence of the strong melodic coloring of verse:

Zhukovsky plays on the harp. *Prolonged passages of sound precede and accompany the words* quietly hummed by the poet, *only for the elucidation of that which he wishes to express with sounds.* Asyndenton, the halt, and reservation are the favorite turns of the poetry of Zhukovsky.[80]

In the system of interaction generated by the dynamics of verse and of speech, there may be semantic gaps, filled up indifferently in the semantic relationship by a word which indicates the dynamics of the rhythm. Undoubtedly, this is where the feature of the choice of words lies. A word sometimes arises according to its significance in verse. Even if the word is "empty" to the highest degree, it acquires a *semblance of meaning* and is "semasiologized" ("semasiologizuetsia"). It is unnecessary to say that the semantics of the word is by its very nature distinguished from its semantics in a prosaic construction, where there is no compactness of the series.

This is why instead of "thought" we have the "value of great thought," or the "equivalent of meaning." Instilled into the verse construction, the indifferent (since it is foreign according to its principal sign) word develops the intensity of oscillating signs instead of the principal sign.

Bessviaznye, strastnye rechi!
Nel'zia v nikh poniat' nichego,
No zvuki pravdivee smysla,
I slovo sil'nee vsego.

Incoherent, passionate speeches!
One cannot understand anything in them,
But sounds are more truthful than sense,
And the word is stronger than all.

This is why words in verse which are intimately connected with an object have such great semantic significance. Where these connections with objects are absent, the principal sign disappears, and in its place may advance a *lexical coloring*. *Oscillating signs* arise in the construction. This applies to *proper names* as well: "The female name in verse is not very real, such as all these Chloes, Lidias, and Delias of the eighteenth century. It is only a title," said Pushkin.[31] And this "title" not only colors verse with a particular image, but may even be predetermined by the construction. The usage of various names with one and the same objective connection, such as "Aonides" and "Camanae," is based on the diverse values of various oscillating signs.

Various cases of the utilization of these oscillating signs are important. They may become a principle of word usage (Novalis). The Symbolists, using words outside their connections and relations to the principal sign of meaning, achieved an *unusual intensity of oscillating signs*. They achieved an "apparent meaning," in which these oscillating signs, strongly coloring the principal ones, appeared as the general semantic background:

V kabakakh, v pereulkakh, v izvivakh,
V elektricheskom sne na iavu,
Ia iskal beskonechno krasivykh
I bessmertno vliublennykh v molvu.

In taverns, in lanes, in windings,
In an electrical day dream,
I searched endlessly for the beautiful
And one immortally in love with common talk.

Into the frame of an ordinary rhythmico-syntactic structure of a stanza are placed seemingly accidental words. A type of semantically open clause is the result of this. The frame "v kabakakh... ia iskal" is filled with secondary members of the clause, *unconnected by their principal signs*. The strength here lies in the stability of the rhythmico-syntactic scheme and the semantic instability of that which fills it. The *compactness* of the series, of the period, and of the stanza receives even greater importance in the presence of this instability. This opens up the possibility, upon the lengthening of the poem, of making the *stanzas*, which are less connected between themselves, broader and more precise. Large verbal masses are not connected between themselves by their principal signs of meaning. At the

94

same time, oscillating signs are intensified, but not to the point of obscuring the principal sign.

In the first line, we have an "ordinary" beginning, as it were, with the utilization of an almost conversational "associative condensation of meaning" (see p. 83 above), preparing for the semantic structure of the following line:

V kabakakh, v pereulkakh, v izvivakh (ulits)...

In taverns, in lanes, in windings (of streets)

In the second line it is easy to trace how the principal signs of the words pale. The group "son naiavu" (literally, a dream while awake—trans.) is a paled oxymoron. Thus, the epithet "electric" and the defined "dream" are not connected by their principal sign, so that *oscillating signs of meaning appear in the epithet.* Upon reunification of the group "v elektricheskom sne" ("in an electrical dream") with the following "naiavu" ("while awake"), the feature of oxymoron is partially renovated by the alteration of one member of the group "son na iavu" ("day-dream").[82] Thus, the oscillating signs of meaning are so intensive in verse that they enlargen to the point of assuming an "apparent meaning," and allow us to pass by this series and turn to the following as if we knew what would occur in it. The sense of each word here is a result of an *orientation toward an adjacent word.*[83]

It is not difficult to observe that the intensifying of oscillating signs is at the same time an intensifying of the semantic feature in verse in general, since it disturbs the habitual semantic environment of the word.

This is why Khlebnikov, who constructs verse according to the principle of combining semantically alien series, thus widely making use of oscillating signs, is semantically more sharp than the "intelligible" epigones of the eighties.

The attitude of the reading public to the "nonsense" of the early Symbolists and early Futurists is curious. The utilization of "apparent semantics" was understood as a setting of riddles. Words which were important in terms of their oscillating signs rather than their principal ones were regarded from the point of view of precisely these principal signs. The particular system of verse semantics was recognized as a semantically communicative system, that is, it was subjected to a consistent solution.

Oscillating signs must be precisely oscillating, apparent semantics precisely apparent. In order for this to occur, the *principal sign in words must be partially retained*, but obscured. The utilization of adjacent words in various combinations is based on this property of "residuals of the principal sign." Principal signs are effaced, but are nevertheless alluded to:

Lilii l 'iutsia, med' blestit,
Solovei stekliannyi poet v kustakh. (N. Tikhonov)

The lilies give off scent, the copper shines,
A nightingale of glass sings in the bushes.

The first line creates a predicate relationship between "lilii" ("lilies") and "l'iutsia" ("give off scent"), so that oscillating signs in both words advance. "Med' " ("copper") is given in combination with "blestit" ("shines"). In the second line, the combination of the two words "steklo" ("glass") and "solovei" ("nightingale") in the form "solovei stekliannyi" ("nightingale" of glass") partially effaces the principal sign in the word "stekliannyi" ("glass") in the postpositive position. This promotes the isolation of oscillating signs in the word "solovei ("nightingale"). Nevertheless, owing to the semantic inertia of the first line, the dimmed principal sign in the word "stekliannyi" ("glass") is retained:

Lilii–med'::solovei–steklo.
Lilies–copper:: nightingale–glass.

In various grammatical relationships, then, series of principal signs are possible which only partially lose their proper role. (Of course, the obscuring of the principal sign may be of varying force.) The usage of an epithet and that which it defines in inverse relation is based on this fact. The epithet and that which it defines change places. Instead of "chuzhuiu dal' "("a foreign distance") we have "dalekuiu chuzh' "("distant foreign place"). Consider M. Delareau's "V chuzh' dalekuiu umchusia" ("In a distant foreign place they whirl") ("Vorozhba"–"Fortune-Telling"). Here the word "chuzh' " ("foreign place") is without a doubt oriented toward "dal' "("distance"). We also have "naemnyi bezvestnik" ("a hired unknown") instead of "bezvestnyi naemnik" ("an obscure hireling"), etc.

If the principal sign were to disappear *completely*, the semantic sharpness of poetic speech would also disappear. (This is why completely transrational language is quickly effaced.)

One should note that *metaphor* and *comparison*, with their collision of principal signs, and with their partial displacement, are also cases where we have the remains of principal signs.

For example:

Kogda zari rumianyi polusvet
V okno tiurmy proshchalnyi svoi privet
Mne, umiraia, posylaet,
I opershis' na zvuchnoe ruzh'e,
Nash chasovoi, pro staroe zhit'e
Mechtaia, stoia zasypaet...

96

When the ruddy twilight of dawn
Into the window of the prison its farewell greeting
To me, dying, sends,
And leaning upon his resounding gun,
Our guard, about the old life
Dreaming, stands dropping off to sleep...

Here the piling on of images is given within the confines of a subordinate clause which fills the entire stanza. The images do not successfully crystallize into whole metaphors. It is interesting that words which are contradictory according to their secondary signs, such as "rumianyi" ("ruddy") on one hand, and "polusvet" ("twilight") and "umiraia" ("dying") on the other, are members of the same image. Actually, the example before us is not so very different from the examples of Blok and Tikhonov which were introduced above. The words are fastened onto a syntactically irreproachable pivot, and from the objective point of view everything is satisfactory. The law of verse and the compactness of the verse series, however, condensed here by the fact that the entire stanza is filled by a subordinate clause and does not present a grammatical whole, has such an influence that this satisfaction proves to be illusory. Meanings of words collide and crowd each other, principal signs of meaning pale, and their *remains* advance. This is especially true of the word "umiraia" ("dying"), which is intonationally brought forward in the line. It acts apart from its own general role in the image (and all the more strongly).

Thus, the phenomenon of "apparent semantics" is based on the compactness of the verse series. With the *almost* complete disappearance of the principal sign, we have the appearance of *"oscillating signs."* These "oscillating signs" create a somewhat *unified group "sense"* outside the semantic connections of the members of the clause.

6. Play on Basic Signs of Meaning

There are, however, cases when this correlation of principal and oscillating sign is changed. This occurs when the oscillating sign receives definition, and with the secondary role of the principal sign comes the *alteration of meaning* (but limited to the given verse system).

Let us examine the end of Zhukovsky's ballad "Allonzo":

Tam v strane preobrazhennykh
Ishchet on svoiu zemnuiu,
Do nego s zemli na nebo
Uletevshuiu podrugu...

Nebesa krugom siiaiut
Bezmiatezhnyi i prekrasny...
I nadezhdoi obol'shchennyi,
Ikh blazhenstva proletaia,

Klichet tam on: Izolina!
I spokoino razdaetsia:
Izolina! Izolina!
Tam, v blazhenstvakh bezotvetnykh.

There in a country of transformations
He seeks his own earthly,
Before him from earth to heaven
Flown away friend...

The heavens around shine
Serene and beautiful...
And by hope deluded,
Their blisses flying past,

He calls there: Izolina!
And peacefully resounds:
Izolina! Izolina!
There, in the blisses of the dumb.

What interests us here is the word "blazhenstva" ("blisses"):

Ikh blazhenstva proletaia...

Their blisses flying past...

Tam, v blazhenstvakh bezotvetnykh...

There in the blisses of the dumb...

Analyzing the signs of meaning which advance in the word, we must admit that the principal sign of the word "blazhenstva" ("blisses") (a blessed, happy state) is quite obscured. In its place advance oscillating signs. With some surprise, we note that the word "blazhenstva" ("blisses") here has a meaning which is somewhat spatial.

The group enslaves the word:

Ikh (nebes) blazhenstva proletaia...

Their (heavens') blisses flying past...

On one hand, the meaning of the word "ikh" ("their"), which is connected
with the word "nebes" ("heavens"), has a progressive influence here. On
the other hand, the word "proletaia" ("flying past") has a regressive influence. The compactness of the connections in the verse series is revealed
in this phenomenon. But the great force of semantic inertia and the assimilative strength of general semantic coloring is also acting here. The word
"ikh" ("their") leads us back across two lines to the first line:

Nebesa *krugom siiaiut.*

The *heavens* around shine.

This word in turn leads us even higher, across two lines to the second
to the last line of the preceding stanza:

Do nego s zemli na nebo...

Before him from earth to *heaven...*

We note the gradual preparation and consolidation of the oscillating sign of
spatiality in the word "blazhenstva" ("blisses")[84] :

Tam v strane *preobrazhennykh,*
Ishchet on svoiu zemnuiu,
Do nego s zemli na nebo
Uletevshuiu *podrugu...*

Nebesa krugom *siiaiut*
Bezmiatezhny i prekrasny...
I nadezhdoi obol'shchenny,
Ikh blazhenstva proletaia,

Klichet tam *on:* Izolina!
I spokoino razdaetsia:
Izolina! Izolina!
Tam, *v* blazhenstvakh *bezotvetnykh.*

There in a country of transformations
He seeks his own earthly,
Before him *from earth to heaven*
Flown away friend...

The heavens around shine
Serene and beautiful...
And by hope deluded,
Their blisses flying past,

He calls *there: Izolina!*
And peacefully *resounds:*
Izolina! Izolina!
There, in the blisses of the dumb.

Thus, we have before us the gradual growth of a spatial coloring, "acting at a distance." In the first line we see "tam v strane" ("there in a country"). In the second line the spatial coloring is acquired by "ischet" ("he seeks"), while in the third line, by "s zemli na nebo" ("from earth to heaven"). In the first line of the second stanza we have "nebesa krugom" ("the heavens around"). (In the word "nebesa" there is an intensification of the spatial nuance.) And at last, in the fourth line we have "ikh blazhenstva proletaia" ("their blisses flying past"). In the first line of the third stanza we see "tam" ("there"), and in the second line "razdaetsia" ("resounds"), which also intensifies the spatial nuance. But in the fourth line "blazhenstva" ("blisses"), already colored by spatiality, is used in a manner parallel with the first line of the first stanza:

Tam, v strane *preobrazhnennykh...*

There, *in a country* of transformations...

Tam, v blazezhenstvakh *bezotvetnykh...*

There, *in the blisses* of the dumb...

One should also note the nuance of spatiality in the intonation of the call:

Klichet tam on: Izolina!
I spokoino razdaetsia:
Izolina! Izolina!

He calls there: *Izolina!*
And peacefully resounds:
Izolina! Izolina!

This call unusually intensifies the general spatial coloring in the stanza. One should also note the important meanings of secondary words: "tam" ("there") and "krugom" ("around").

And so, in the last line the oscillating sign of spatiality in the meaning of the word "blazhenstva" ("blisses") is consolidated (by means of the principal sign being partially obscured).

However, among the factors promoting such an alteration of meaning, the formal element of the word played quite a major role. The formal element in the word undoubtedly carries important semantic functions. (Consider Rozwadowski's "law of the binomiality of meaning.")

The fact of the matter is that the suffix "-stvo" (the singular of blazhenstva" being "blazhenstvo"—trans.), having a qualitative significance, significantly promotes this meaning connected with the sign of spatiality. The suffix "-stvo" generates substantive qualities. ("Some nouns retaining this meaning receive a collective significance when applied to many persons: panstwo, in the sense of 'the state.' "[85]) There occurs even further evolution of collectiveness toward spatiality: "tsarstvo" ("kingdom"), "kniazhestvo" ("principality"), "gertsogstvo" ("dukedom"), "khanstvo" ("khanate"), "grafstvo" ("county"), "mark-grafstvo" ("margravedom"), "abbatstvo" ("abbey"), "namestnichestvo" ("viceregency"), "lesnichestvo" ("forestry"), "gradonachal'stvo" ("borough"), "voevodstvo" ("province"), "arkhiere-istvo" ("bishropric"), "general-gubernatorstvo" ("general-governorship"), "prostranstvo" ("space"), and "bratstvo" ("fraternity) in occasional application, such as in Shevchenko:

A yz bracva te bursactvo
Movchky vyhladane.

And from brotherhood that bursactvo†
Silently he looks.

(†"bursactvo" student body of a "bursa," a boarding-house for theology students)

The suffix "-stvo" in the word "blazhenstvo" ("bliss") does not, understandably, have this coloring, but it is quite easily associated with the "-stvo" which does have it, and even replaced by it.

It is curious that the original peem of Uhland's is devoid of both resources. The feature of the *growth* of the spatial sign is quite narrowed in terms of general coloring, and the formal element does not play a role:

Schon im Lande der verklärten
Wacht'er auf, und mit Verlangen
Sucht er seine süsse Freundin,
Die er wähnt vorangegangen;

Aller Himmel lichte Räume
Sieht er herrlich sich verbreiten;

"Blanka! Blanka!" ruft er sehnlich
Durch die öden Seligkeiten.

In a land of transformation
He watches, and with longing
He searches for his sweet friend,
Whom he believes has gone before him;

All the heavens are shining
He sees it glorious and splendid;
"Blanka! Blanka!" he calls passionately
Through the barren blisses.

The meaning of the word "Seligkeiten" ("blisses") proves to be so unprepared for that the editor attached the following note to the poem: "Durch die für ihn öden Räume des Reiches der Seligen" ("For him, the barren space of the state of bliss").[86]

7. Lexical Coloring in Verse

The *lexical* sign of meaning is found as well in the distinctive conditions of verse. The unity and compactness of the verse series, the dynamization of the word in verse, and the successiveness of verse speech totally distinguish the very *structure* of verse vocabulary from the structure of prosaic vocabulary.

First of all, in view of the work's verse significance, the lexical sign advances *more strongly;* hence, the enormous importance of each transient lexical coloring of the most secondary words in verse. One might say that each word in verse has a distinctive *lexical tone.* Owing to the compactness of the verse series, which increases the contaminating and assimilating force of lexical coloring on the entire verse series, a unity of *lexical tonality* is created as the unfolding of the verse is first strengthened, and then weakened and altered.

Finally, the *unity* of the verse series, which emphasizes *boundaries,* is a strong means for the isolation of lexical tone.

At the same time, in verse is observed the distinctive correlation of the lexical sign of meaning, as a constant secondary sign, with the principal sign of meaning on one side, and with the specifics of oscillating verse signs on the other.

The lexical sign does not displace the oscillating signs.

We will turn our attention to the particular role which dialectisms, or simply words of the conversational language play in verse. Their *novelty* and their strong *action* in verse, which is not observed in prose, needs to be

102

attributed to the verse significance of the word, and to the performance of oscillating signs. Unfamiliarity or incomplete familiarity with the word plays an important role. Cases of complete misunderstanding of a word are possible, i.e., *a lack of knowledge of the principal sign* which are, of course, even more conducive to the performance of oscillating signs.

This and other aspects of the *principal sign* are decisive for lexical selection.

Thus, use of complex adjectives (*composita*) distinguishes all of the archaists. Lomonosov called these "attractions." The abundant use of "attractions" (by Zhukovsky and Tyutchev) is always an index of the archaist tendency.[87] Not only is the selection of epithets interesting,[88] but also the *semantic stream* brought with them. Without question, what we face here is a case of the most intimate influence of two words. Various cases, of course, are possible, depending on which parts of speech are present and in what order they enter into the connection (conjunction—adjective; noun—adjective; adjective—adjective, etc.), how common their usage, and how strong the connection (confluence, or only combination and rapproachment). This always results in the greatest interaction of principal signs, and *oscillating signs* may advance. This happens particularly in the case of the combination or rapproachment of words with remote principal signs: Zhukovsky's "bespyl'no-efirnyi" ("dustlessly-ethereal"), or Tyutchev's "dymnolegko" ("smokily-lightly") or mglisto-lileino" ("hazily-lily-white").[89]

This special use of complex and double adjectives is characteristic of the school of archaists, with their usual obscuring of the principal signs, and the advancement of oscillating signs.

The reason complex and double adjectives are such a defined device in verse lies in the significance which they attach to the secondary second member of the verse *composita*. It also emphasizes the intimacy of their connection and contiguity. (The same factor promotes the selection of syntactic turns in verse, such as the *inversion,* particularly at the end of series, which is an agreement with the principle of the *compactness of the series.*[90]

An interesting play on principal signs may occur when the word is carried at once by two lexical series, and is connected with two principal signs. In context, then, oscillating signs advance *in connection with the other principal sign.*

Consider Blok:

> *Ty* otoshla—*i ia v pustyne*
> *K pesku goriachemu prinik.*

> *You have gone*—and I am in the wilderness
> Pressed against the fiery sand.

The word "otoshla" ("have gone away") is carried at once by two lexical series: Russian and Old Church Slavic, and carries different principal signs. "Otoiti" (the infinitive of "otoshla"–trans.) may either mean "umeret' " ("to have passed away") or "uiti" ("to go away"). In the present case (at the beginning of the poem) it is not clear which principal sign advances in the context. The meaning seems *to oscillate between the two principal signs*, whereas the subsequent vocabulary does not create a favorable surrounding for association with the Church Slavonic vocabulary:

Ty otoshla–*i ia v pustyne*
K pesku goriachemu prinik.
No slova gordogo otnyne
Ne mozhet vymolvit' iazyk
...Syn chelovecheskii ne znaet,
Gde preklonit' emu glavu.

You have gone—and I am in the wilderness
Pressed against the fiery sand.
But *from now on* the proud word
The tongue cannot utter.
...*The Son of Man does not know,*
Where to lay his head.

It goes without saying that the oscillating sign remains here, even after the principal sign has been determined.

Another example of the above is the use of a word with two different lexical characteristics, and accordingly, two principal signs. Consider Tyutchev:

V nochi lazurnoi pochivaet Rim.
Vzoshla luna i ovladela im,
I spiashchii grad bezliudno velichavyi
Napolnila svoei bezmolvnoi slavoi.

In the azure night Rome sleeps.
The moon has ascended and taken possession of it,
And the uninhabited stately sleeping city
Was filled with its own speechless *glory.*

Here the word "slava" ("glory") may be conveyed at once by two lexical series: as an archaism and a "biblicalism." It is connected with two principal signs. First, it coincides with the Russian use of the word. Secondly, it has a specific character: "they kept awake and saw his *glory*" (Luke 9, 32); "we have beheld his *glory*" (John I, 14); " and manifested his own *glory*" (John 2, 11);"*you* would see the *glory* of God" (John11,40); "because he saw his *glory*" (John 12,41); "the appearance of his *glory*" (Peter 4, 13); " because of the glory on his face" (2 Corinthians 3,7); "we all with unveiled face reflect the *glory of God*, in that the same image is transformed from *glory* to *glory*" (2 Corinthians 3, 18); "the radiance of *glory*" (Hebrews 1, 3); "and the temple was filled with the smoke from the *glory* of God" (Revelation 15, 8). Thus, "glory" has, in the above examples, the objective coloring of the principal sign (*"I see* his glory"; "the radiance of *glory*"; "the temple was filled with the *smoke* from the glory of God").

It is interesting how this principal sign is prepared by Tyutchev:

> Napolnila svoei bezmolvnoi *slavoi.*
> *Was filled with its own speechless* glory.

Nevertheless, the principal sign of the Russian lexical environment is retained as an oscillating sign in the word "slava" ("glory").

We should, however, recognize that *the strength of the lexical coloring is in direct opposition to clarity of the principal sign*: the strongest cases of lexical coloring occur with the obscuring of the principal sign:

> Sasha raised her eyebrows and began *loudly in a sing-song voice:* "When they had departed, an angel of the Lord appeared to Joseph in a dream and said, 'Rise up and take the child and his mother...' " "The child and his mother," repeated Olga and then flushed from nervousness.
> " 'And flee to Egypt, and wait there until ("dondezhe") the...' " *At the word "until" ("dondezhe") Olga could not restrain herself and began to cry.* In Maria's eyes tears appeared, and then in the eyes of the sister of Ivan Makarych. (Chekhov, "The Peasants")

The greatest lexical coloration here falls on the *unknown* word, with complete absence of a principal sign.

In a more complex example, we could see how the lexical coloring advances at the expense of the principal sign and vice versa.

Concerning metaphor, or "rhetorical words," in the first edition of the *Rhetoric*, no. 83 of part II, Lomonosov says:

> Instead of the peculiar words which the thing or action really means, often other things or actions are relied on from a similar situation which can be used. For example, 1. when a word belonging to an in-organic thing is transferred to an organic thing, such as the 'solid man' instead of 'miserly,' or *the regiments run to battle, instead of* they go...[91]

Here Lomonosov has employed a "biblicalism." Consider the following:

"who ran in despair" (1 Corinthians 9, 24); "and one of them ran to him (Matthew 27,48); "and one ran" (Mark 15, 36); "and ran and fell on him" (Luke 15, 20); "and ran to tell his disciples" (Matthew 28, 8), etc. In other words, we see "run" *in the sense of "to escape, to break into a run"* ("currere," "procurrere").[92]

Thus, the use of the words "polki tekut na bran' " ("the regiments run to battle") has for Lomonosov a double purpose: 1. as a metaphor, a collision of two principal signs, where the word is conveyed by the Russian lexical series; 2. the well-known lexical coloring of the elevated style, the word being recognized as belonging to the "biblical vocabulary."

While both of these were present at the beginning, the "elevated metaphor" was also present. Because of the habitualness of the collision, the principal sign in the word "tekut" ("run") is effaced.[93] The metaphor was effaced, but it has not become lingual and current because of this. Rather, the *lexical* coloring has advanced more clearly:

> *I on poslushno vput'potek*
> *I k utru vozvratilsia s iadom.   (Pushkin, "Antsar," 1828)*

> And he obediently *ran* on the path
> And toward morning he returned with the poison.
> > ("The Upas Tree")

Each *revival of a metaphor* inevitably weakens this lexical coloring. The stronger the revival, the weaker this coloring:

> *Kuda* tekut *naroda shumny volny?*

> Where do the noisy waves of people *run?*

Here the principal sign is strengthened by the introduction of the word "waves," and the word is carried in a single lexical series. There is no place for the biblical coloring since the principal sign is still alive.

Therefore, *words without a principal sign* (in a given linguistic environment) will be the strongest in terms of lexical coloring. Unintelligible dialectisms are typical here. (Consider Tolstoy's "golomia," or the many unintelligible dialectisms of Remizov, Klyuev, or Vs. Ivanov.) Also consider unintelligible "biblicalisms" ("dondezhe") ("until") and unintelligible barbarisms, such as the following of Vyazemsky:

> *Umizgać się! Za eto slovo*
> *Khotia usham ono surovo,*
> *Ia rad ves' nash slovar' otdat'.   ("Stantsiia," 1828)*

Umizgać sie!† For this word
Though it is severe on the ears
I am glad to give up our dictionary.   ("The Station")

(†Polish for, "to court, to woo.")
    Proper names, which retain their lexical coloring quite strongly, should be discussed here:

> *Vse ne o tom prozrachnaia tverdit,*
> *Vse lastochka, podruzhka,* Antigona...
> *...Nichego,* golubka Evridika,
> *Chto u nas studenaia zima...*

> It is nothing if hardens the limpid,
> Swallow, friend, *Antigone...*
> ...It does not matter, *dove Eurydice,*
> That we have a very cold winter...

    Here the lexical coloring of the words "lastochka" ("swallow") and "podruzhka" ("friend") and of the word "Antingona" ("Antigone") are connected by their opposition of lexical elements. The same is true of "golubka Evridika" ("dove Eurydice").
    The use of foreign names in verse is based on this. Consider the Alexandrines. Also consider Ronsard's "antiquated tonality":

> *Ah! que je suis marry que ma Muse francoise*
> *Ne peut dire ces mots comme fait la Grégoise:*
> *Ocymore, Dyspotme, Oligochronien,*
> *Certes, je les dirois du Sang Valésian.*
> > ("Le Tombeau de Marguerite de France
> > de Savoye")

> Ah! but I am sad that my French muse
> Cannot say such words as the Greek
> Ocymore, Dyspotme, Oligochronien,
> Of course, I've said them but out of tune.
> > ("The Tomb of Marguerite of France,
> > Duchess of Savoy")

    Consider Boileau ("barbaric tonality" as compared with "antiquated"):

> *La fable offre à l'esprit mille agrémens divers:*
> *Là tous les noms heureaux semblent nés pour les vers,*
> *Ulysse, Agamemnon, Oreste, Idoménée,*

Helene, Menelas, Paris, Hector, Enee.
O le plaisant projet d'un poete ignorant,
Qui de tant de heros va choisir Childebrand!
D'un seul nom quelquefois le son dur bizarre
Rend un poeme entier ou burlesque ou barbare.
                                        (L'art Poetique, Chant III)

The fable offers the spirit a thousand different pleasures:
All these blissful names *appear made for verse,*
Ulysses, Agamemnon, Orestes, Idomenee,
Helen, Menelau, Paris, Hektor, Enee.
Oh what a ridiculous project for an uninstructed poet
That would dare to choose as a hero *Childebrand!*
The harsh or peculiar sound of a single name
May render an entire poem either burlesque or barbarous!

Consider the frequent use of the *catalogue of names* by the Karamzinians (a device coming to them from the French poets), such as that of Dmitriev:

Biuffon, Russo, Mabli, Kornelii,
Ves' Shakespir, ves' Pop i Gium,
Zhurnaly Adissona, Stilia,
I vse Didota, Berskervilia.   *("Puteshestvie N.N. v Parizh")*

Buffon, Rousseau, Mably, Corneille,
All Shakespeare, all Pope and Hume,
The journals of Addison and Steele,
And all of Diderot and Baskerville. ("Journey of N.N. to Paris")

Here we see an example of the above with a poem of Pushkin's:

Prochel on Gibbona, Russo,
Manzoni, Gerdera, Shamfora,
Madame de Stael, Bisha, Tisso... (Eugene Onegin, VII, 35*)*

He read Gibbon, Rousseau,
Manzoni, Herder, Chamfort,
Madame de Stael, Bichat, Tissot...

Whereas in the above examples the *lexical tonality* is important for the most part, the Symbolists have made use of the catalogue of names mainly because of the oscillating signs which advance in verse. Consider Montesquiou:

Centrenthus, Areca, Tegestas, Muscaris,
Messanbrianthemum et Strutiopberis,
Arthurium, Rhapis, Arecas et Limanthe...

Here we already have a phenomenon which turns into the "transrational," but nevertheless retains its lexical tonality.

We turn now to a less forceful, more typical example. Consider Pushkin:

Krasy Lais, *zavetnye piry*
I kliki radosti bezumnoi,
I mirnkyh muz minutnye dary,
I lepetan'e slavy shumnoi...   ("V.F. Raevskomu," 1822)

The beauties of *Laises,* sacred feasts
And cries of reckless gladness,
And of the peaceful muses momentary gifts,
And the babbling of noisy glory.   ("To V.F. Raevsky")

Here it is as though the principal lexical tone in the word "Lais" ("Laises") were given us. The word "krasa, krasy" ("beauty," "beauties") had for Pushkin a definite secondary sign with a partial preservation of the principal sign:

Tak, na prodazhnuiu krasu,
Nasytias' eiu toroplivo...

So, to a corrupt beauty,
Sated with her quickly...

In the combination "krasy Lais" ("beauties of Laises") this secondary sign is present, but together with this usage an original lexical coloring has advanced.

This lexical tonality of proper names was realized by Vyazemsky when he wrote:

Orlov, Potemkin, Rumianstsov, and Suvorov had in them as well something particularly poetic and lyric. Their well-composed names have added some harmony to Russian verse. There can be no doubt that Derzhavin knew this and left evidence of this in one of the lines from his "The Waterfall" ("Vodopad"):
...Ekaterina vozrydala!

...Catherine sobbed!

Verse composed of a proper name and a verb has... an elevated poetic feeling. This verse is without a doubt exceptional Russian verse, but also it is a *Russian picture*. The fortunate poet who wishes to profit by this means must be able to divine an impression and to srtike a flame in poetry from the combination of two words.[94]

The assimilating force of lexical coloring in verse is made clear in the following example:

> *Kogda sred' orgii zhizni shumnoi*
> *Menia postignul* ostrakizm,
> *Uvidel ia tolpy bezumnoi*
> *Prezrennyi, robkii* egoizm.   (Pushkin, "F.N. Glinke," 1822)

> When amidst the noisy orgies of life
> *Ostracism* had befallen me,
> I saw the reckless crowd's
> Contemptible, timid *egotism*.   ("To F.N. Glinka")

The word "egoizm" ("egotism") is, of course, a "barbarism" in Pushkin's dictionary, with a clear, prosaic coloring:

> ....Takov moi organism.   ·
> Izvol'te men prostit' nenuzhnyi prozaiazm.

> ....*Such is my organism.*
> *Forgive me the unnecessary prosaism.*

The word "ostrakizm" ("ostracism") which precedes it is clear lexically, not as a prosaism, but as a "greekism." It not only lexically colors the material side of the word, but also the formal. The suffix "-ism," precisely because of the lexical clarity of the material side, is also recognized as a "greekism." The word "ostrakism" ("ostracism") is the first rhyming member in the rhyme "ostrakizm"–"egoizm" ("ostracism"–"egotism"). The rhymed connection here is given via the formal side of the word. The "Greek" suffix of the word "ostrakism" ("ostracism") calls forth the same lexical coloring in the suffix of the word "egoizm" ("egotism"). The entire word is thereby colored anew. Because of the "prosaism," "egoism" ("egotism") is recolored a "greekism."

This lexical coloring is formed not only in a progressive sequence, but also in a regressive sequence. The word "orgii"("orgies"), which is lexically semi-effaced, is also more strongly colored lexically owing to the word "ostrakizm" ("ostracism").

This lexical coloring is a very important factor in the unfolding of the

110

lyrical plot. The tone, which is given with some strength in this relationship with the word, sometimes predetermines not only the lexical formation of the entire piece, but even the direction of its plot:

1. *Nel'zia, moi tolstyi* Aristipp:
   Khot' ia liubliu tvoi besedy,
   Tvoi milyi nrav, tvoi milyi khrip,
   Tvoi vkus i zhirnye obedy,
   No ne mogu s toboi plyt'
   K bregam poludennoi Tavridy.
   Proshu menia ne pozabyt,'
   Liubimets Vakkha i Kipridy!
2. *Kogda chakhotochnyi otets*
   Nemnogo toshchei Eneidy
   Puskalsia v more nakonets,
   Emu Goracii, *umnyi l'stets,*
   Prislal torzhestvennuiu odu,
   Gde drugu Avgustov pevets
   Sulil khoroshuiu pogodu:
   No Is'tivykh od ia ne pishu,—
   Ty ne v chakhote, slav bogu:
   U neba ia tebe proshu
   Lish'appetita na dorogu. (Pushkin, "Davydovu")

1. It is impossible, my stout *Aristippe:*
   Though I love your conversations,
   Your sweet disposition, your sweet wheeze,
   Your manner and rich dinners,
   I cannot sail with you
   To the shore of the southern *Tauric.*
   Allow me not to forget,
   Favorite of *Bacchus and Cupid!*
2. When the consumptive father
   Of the slightly emaciated Aeneas
   Set out to sea at last,
   To him *Horace,* clever flatterer,
   Sent a festive ode,
   Where to a friend of *Augustus* the singer
   Promised good weather;
   But flattering odes I will not write,—
   You are not in consumption, praise God:
   From heaven I request for you
   Only appetites on the journey. ("To Davydov")

111

In the first line, strong lexical coloring is given in the word "Aristippe," which is applied to the entire stanza. In the following stanza there is a renewal of this lexical characteristic: "Tavridy" ("Tauric") and "Vakkha i Kipridy" ("Bacchus and Cupid"). What follows is *lexically* connected to this by the unfolding of the lyrical plot:

> *Kogda chakhotochnyi otets*
> *Nemnogo toshchei* Eneidy...

> When the consumptive father
> Of the slightly emaciated *Aeneas*...

The general lexical connection here justifies and motivates the feature of the sudden displacement: 1. Aristippe; 2. father of Aeneas.

In all of the examples quoted above, what is important, of course, is something I have already mentioned: lexical coloring advances more strongly with the disappearance of the principal sign. The general lexical affiliation replaces, as it were, the individual principal sign.

Here we should take into account that the use of words with an effaced principal sign results in a stronger advancement of *oscillating signs*, which join with the sign of lexical coloring.

The lexical coloring in a given case may serve as a type of justification or motivation for the engagement of words which are foreign according to their principal sign.

In saying this, it follows that the investigation of lexical coloring and lexical tonality of verse, and therefore of the correlation of the lexical sign with the principal sign and oscillating sign, should be combined. Under various conditions of verse and prose, lexical signs have varying strengths and varying functions.

(Precisely for this reason, we need to take into consideration the lexical intensity of the dictionary itself: both neologisms and archaisms, etc., may be of varying strengths, of varying levels of "novelty" or "antiquity.")

8. The Influence of "Instrumentation" on the Sense of Words

The principal and secondary signs of meaning, on one hand, and the material and formal part of the word, on the other, are distinct concepts which do not overlap each other, as I said above. The concept of the principal sign and of secondary signs is distributed throughout the entire word, i.e., throughout the unity of its material and formal parts. Understandably, some separate alterations in meaning, whether in the material or formal part of the word, may result in alterations of principal and secondary signs, by

112

influencing the advancement of oscillating signs in the word.

In this area of a partial alteration of the meanings of the material and formal parts of the word, there are two factors of rhythm which operate: *rhyme and instrumentation*. The action of the first is based on the unity of the series, and the second, on the compactness of the series.

The correlation between the material and formal parts of the word, or so-called "instrumentation," which is one of the factors of rhythm, plays an especially   important and insufficiently studied role in this alteration.

The concept of "instrumentation," as well as the term itself, is quite vague it is already preconditioned by the musical character of the phenomenon, but this does not exhaust the matter. By instrumentation, then, one may understand a general phonetic consistency and a general phonetic coloring of verse.

The name "instrumentation" is given to anything which is advanced in the general articulatory (and acoustic) background of the group—*sound repetitions* ("povtory"), according to the terminology of Brik. This seems to me the sole legitimate modern approach. The actual rhythmical factors are the phonetic elements which are advanced against the general articulatory background, and by the strength of their advancement, capable of assuming a rhythmical role. I repeat that the rhythmical role of sound repetition ("povtor") is inadequate for such a purpose as meter. The dynamic grouping produced by meter is accomplished via a progressive—regressive path, the decisive feature here being the progressive. (Consider the importance of the *metrical impulse* in *vers libre*). Instrumentation, meanwhile, as a rhythmical factor, unites into groups via a *regressive* path. (The progressive feature here is not eliminated, for with obvious and monotonous instrumentation, the feature of phonetic anticipation might well play an essential role. This role, however, is secondary in comparison with the role of the regressive feature). Sound repetitions ("povtory") organize rhythmical groups regressively. (The greatest rhythmical stress, therefore, lies on the posterior member of the group.) Thus, in speaking about instrumentation, it would not do to speak about its equivalents in the shape of a dynamic impulse. The creation of equivalents is revealed in the breadth of the linking sign from the phonetic point of view. For the realization of the rhythmical role of instrumentation, *the most general signs of the phonetic kinship of sounds are sufficient*.

In posing the question in this way, the following begin to play an important role in sound repetitions ("povtory"): 1. the proximity or compactness of the sound repetitions: 2. their correlation with meter; 3. the quantitative factor (the quantity of sounds and their group character); 4. the qualitative factor (the quality of the sound); 5. the quality of the repeated verbal element (material or formal); 6. the nature of words united by instrumentation.

The greater the proximity of sound repetitions ("povtory"), the clearer their rhythmical role. The scattering of sound repetitions at a considerable distance may be considered as a *preparatory* factor, establishing a particular phonetic base, or as a factor of "dynamic preparation" (realized, however, only in the presence of the license of intimate and obvious sound repetitions).

This factor is combined with other factors. *Correlation with the meter* is the most important of them. When metrical articulations coincide with a phonetic grouping, then sound repetitions ("povtory") usually play the role of secondary groupings within metrical groups:

> *Ferrara, furii/i zavisti zmiia* (Batiushkov).

> Ferrara, the fury and envies of a snake.

> *Vyshib dno/i vyshel von* (Pushkin).

> Knocked out the bottom/and went out there.

This is related to the great significance of accentual groups.

The sign of the *quantity* of sound is also important. This is easy to observe, since sound repetitions of a single sound organizes speech less than sound repititions of groups. With regard to semantics, it is exceptionally important what kind of groups are repeated. *Groups of initial sounds* of a word receive the greatest semantic significance. The phenomenon of "the unexpected" is based on the semantic coloration of these initial groups. This consists of giving us the first syllable of a particular word which we expect, but then completing the word with what is not expected. This is a favorite device of Aristophanes.[95]

It is also important whether the repetition is complete or only partial. With partial sound repetitions, the sounds which distinguish groups play a special role, so that the second group may be recognized as a variant of the first. The last two factors in the semantic relationship are hardly unimportant. They are the quality of sounds and the relationship of sound to the word, i.e., the affiliation of the sounds with either the material or formal verbal element.

The acoustic and articulatory coloring of verse depends upon the acoustic and articulatory wealth or poverty of sound repetitions ("povtory"). However, even articulatory and acoustic poverty does not completely exclude the *rhythmical role of sound repetitions* or the realization of its being weak in the indicated relationships. (It is a type of "negative sign," which can be quite strong depending on the character of surrounding groups.)

The theory of the eighteenth century was aware of the rhythmical role of instrumentation (consider Bobrov and Shishkov), but understood it exclusively in terms of onomatopoeia. Because of this, Shishkov came to the conclusion that all poetry is like onomatopoeia. Modern theory willingly pauses at the concept of "phonetic metaphor."[96]

Both onomatopoeia and phonetic metaphors are met, of course, in great quantity. It not only follows, therefore, to blend them together, but also to insist on the *semantic clarity and synonymy of these devices*. We should not overlook the fact that onomatopoeia and phonetic metaphors are not sensed as a type of appendage. They are not oil floating on water, but rather they enter into *definite correlations with the meanings of words*. This correlation and deformation of semantics may be such a strong feature in itself that the specific characteristic of onomatopoeia and phonetic metaphor may be covered up to a large degree. Only an analysis of what this deformation in each separate case consists of may elucidate the role of instrumentation, which varies according to its functions.

Let us take some examples of phonetic metaphor:

> *I v sumu ego pustuiu*
> *Suiut gramotu druguiu.*   (Pushkin, "Skazka o tsare Saltane")

And into his empty pouch
They shove another decree. ("Tale of Tsar Saltan")

> *Lomit on u duba suk*
> *I v tugoi sgibaet luk.*
> *So kresta snurok shelkovyi*
> *Natianul na luk dobovyi,*
> *Tonku trostochku slomil...*   (same as above)

He breaks a branch off the oak
And bends it into a strong bow.
From the cross the silken cord
He strung on the oaken bow,
A thin twig he broke off...

Here we should note that the first line corresponds to the second line via the group "su": "sumu" ("pouch")–"suiut" ("shove"). There is an incomplete repetition (*reduplication*) in the word "pustuiu" ("empty"). The exceptional phonetic expressiveness of the verse depends here on the labialization of the sound "u." The repetition of this sound makes its articulation even more perceptible because of the fact that these repetitions do not give the sound in a monotonous form, but rather in alterations of various nuances. This alternation of articulatory variants gives the sensation of *protraction* of the articulation.

Before us is the phenomenon of the *phonetic gesture*, which quite persuasively prompts real gestures. We need only note that *concrete* and simple gestures are not prompted here.

The meaning of words is strongly deformed. The principal sign of the word "sumu" ("pouch") is connected syntactically and phonetically with the word "pustuiu" ("empty"). It is connected regressively with the word "suiut" ("shove") in the following line. It is as though the principal sign were obscured, retreating before the revived *oscillating signs*.

Thus, not only does the general semantic coloring of the series act here, but also the *displacement of the meaning of the word*, which is a result of its intimate rhythmical connection with other words.

Let us take an example of onomatopoeia:

> *Katitsia ekho po goram,*
> *Kak grom, gremiashchii po gromam.*

> The echo rolls along the mountains,
> Like thunder, thundering in a thundery way.

The characteristic feature here is not only the repetition of a definite phonetic group, but also the repetition of *the base of one and the same word*. Thus, the entire group presents its own pnonetic sound repetition ("povtor") *via the unity of the material part of the words*. Without a doubt, this strengthens the material part so that onomatopoeia becomes, in the given case, an intricate complex. It bears the action of the emotional quality of the sound and the amplification of the meaning of the material part of the word. The amplification of this meaning comes with the series, and depends upon the syntactic correlation *of words with a single base. The words are realized* as articulated parts of a single whole. The syntactic hierarchy of words and the variants of the material part of the word acquire special significance. This syntactic frame and these variations and alterations— "grom" ("thunder") and "gremiashchii" ("thundering")— create, as it were, *the protracted and dismembered action of a single material part*. This is why the repetition of one and the same word in identical form is a weak deforming device, and an even weaker rhythmical device. The latter depends upon the fact that such identity is a characteristic rhythmical device of practical speech, and is associated with it.[97] The former we might compare with the alteration or variation of sounds in onomatopoetic doublings: "Zikzack," "whirr-warr" (Fr. "pele-mele"), "Schnikschnak," "krimskrams," "Wischiwaschi," "Kling-klang," "Mischmasch,""fickfack," "gickgack," "kliffklaff," "klippklapp," "klitschklatsch," "klimperklamper."[98]

Whereas in onomatopoeia this intensifies only the general group semantics, the operation of the feature of "ablaut" (that is, the variation of sounds and the feature of alteration, with the intensifying of general material parts) gives a distinct coloring to separate words.

Consider Khlebnikov:

O, zasmeites', smekhachi,
O, usmeites', smekhachi.
Chto smeiutsia smekhami,
Chto smeianstvuiut smeial'no.
Smeshiki, smeshiki,
Smekhunchiki, smekhunchiki.
O, zasmeites', smekhachi,
O, usmeites' smekhachi.

Oh, laugh, laughers,
Oh, laugh it off, laughers,
They that laugh with laughs,
They will laugh laughingly.
Laughsters, laughsters,
Laughingers, laughingers,
Oh, laugh, laughers,
Oh, laugh it off, laughers.

Here, of course, one could speak of the intensification of the general meaning, and of the quite strong semantic role of individual words, such as "smekhachi" ("laughers"), "smeshiki" ("laughsters"), etc. Thus, in view of the importance of the semantic frame, a differentiation of words with a single material part which are placed next to each other in the relationship of members of a clause, the *formal* elements of the word become important. The more the material part of words coincide, the more clearly their semantics advance. This coincidence condemns the individual material part of each word to comparative colorlessness. Its meaning is absorbed by the general meaning. Only *variants* of the material part advance more clearly, so that the meaning of *suffixes* is much stronger. As a result of this, we receive 1. the meaning of the general material part, and 2. the individual and clear, formal characteristic of each separate word.

Here is another example:

Zatikhla tishe tishina. (Derzhavin)

The quiet quieted down more quietly.

Here we have a complex phenomenon in which a phonetic metaphor is present:

tikh—tish—tish

It recedes into the background, however, before the threefold repetition of one and the same root, with variation and dissimilarity of formal elements, and with the hierarchy of the words as members of a clause. Because of this, the whole group is recognized as a *dismembered whole*, in which each word is semantically strong and colored (as a result of the whole), and also has its own proper formal sign and role in the clause. The *feature of distinction*, in the given case, is as strong as the feature of similarity. Thus, even here we must examine the character of sound repetitions ("povtory") in relationship to the element of the word, i.e., whether the material or formal part of the word is involved.

In the first case, the phenomena are interesting in which the material part is not repeated, but made to resemble another material part:

I ten' *nakhmurilas'* temnei.

And the *shade* was overcast *more darkly*.

The material part of the word "ten'" ("shade") is colored by its connection with the word "temnei" ("more darkly"). This creates the *illusion* of a "revival of the principal sign." Of course, such a revival is not a revival, but rather a *new coloring*. Compare this example with the following:

1. *Unylaia pora*, ochei ocharovan'e.

1. A sad time, *the charm of the eyes*.

2. *Stoit odin vo* vse vselennoi.

2. Stands alone in *all the universe*.

"Ochei ocharovan'e" ("the charm of the eyes") is a metrically and phonetically united group. This is realized with the comparison of the sounds "ochei" and "ocha." Here we have two consecutive features: the feature of recognition of elements of the previous word in the word "ocharovan'e" ("charm"), and the feature of the unification of both words into a group. As a result, the material part of the word "ocharovan'e" ("charm") is colored through the strong connection with the material part of the word "ochei" ("eyes"). This occurs as the first stage of the redistribution of the material and formal part (*irradition*, according to the terminology of Bréale). It is as though we derived "ocharovan'e" ("charm") from the root of "ochi" ("eyes"). This is also true to a significant degree of the second example. The first syllable in the word "vselennoi" ("universe") is connected with the preceding word "vse" ("all"). The same partial process of the redistribution of the formal and material part of the word occurs: "vse-lennoi."

Thus, the oscillating signs of meaning come to life in the word, which in the strongest cases may result in a *false etymology*. That which in spoken language occurs under conditions of maximum coincidence may occur under conditions of incomplete coincidence in verse, with its unusually strong and habitual associative connections.

Habitual devices of instrumentation may actually cause habitual images.

Consider the selection of images by Lomonosov:

> *Odnako,* rod rossiiskii *znal...*
> Rossiiskii rod *i plod Petrov...*
> *Krasuisia svetlo,* rosskii rod...
> Spasenny dnes' rossiiskii rod...

> However, the *Russian family* knew...
> The *Russian family* and fruit of Peter...
> It is colored brightly, *a luxurious family...*
> Life-saving day the *Russian family...*

It is interesting to note that Lomonosov "semasiologized" syllables. Consider from his grammar, no. 106:

> At the beginning (of a word), consonants depend upon the subsequent vowel. With these are begun any word in the Russian language. The same is true concerning the sequence of vowels. For example: "u-zhasnyi" ("terrible"), "chu-dnyi" ("wonderful"), "dria-khlyi" ("decrepit"), "topchu" ("I trample down"). The words "sneg" ("snow"), "dno" ("bottom"), "khleb" ("bread"), and "pchela" ("bee") begin with the consonants "sn-," "dn-," "khl-," and "pch-."[99]

The selection of images might also be conditioned by "false etymology." Consider the root-word of Tredyakovsky and Shishkov. This "root-word" can be realized as artistic creation. Consider Khlebnikov's "declension of words."

Consider Nyrop:

> Phonetic harmony unites words into indissoluble groups. It protects the old words and forms from destruction, as well as creating new forms when the consonance does not succeed. It determines the selection of words and decides what images and comparisons will be most useful. Therefore, its role is not exclusively of a formal nature. In joining words with one another, it also joins their ideas."[100]

The role of phonetic repetitions, which give rise to oscillating signs of meaning (by means of redistribution of the material and formal parts of the word), and which convert speech into a single correlative whole, compels us to examine them as a distinctive *rhythmical metaphor.*

9. Influence of Rhyme on the Sense of Words

Rhyme is quite an important semantic lever. The condition of rhyme lies in the progressive action of the first member and the regressive action of the second member.

Therefore, all factors which secure the strength of any of the following are important: 1. the relationship of rhyme to meter and syntax (of which I spoke above), 2. the proximity or compactness of the rhymed members, 3. the quantity of the rhymed members, 4. the quality of the rhymed verbal element as a specific condition in relationship to semantics (material-formal, formal-formal, etc.). If the rhyme is important as a rhythmical factor, and the presensation of the end of a series or period is connected with it, then we must note that in relationship to the semantic action of the rhyme, the factor of proximity or compactness acquires a great importance. This is why in paired verses (Alexandrians, for example) this action will be stronger than in stanzas with remote rhymes. This is also why the absolute quantity of the series is important here. In a short series, rhyme will be stronger than in a long one.

The progressive action of the first member is expressed in the isolation of the second, and sometimes in its partial anticipation. In the latter case, the area of play on habitual associations is revealed. In this relationship, the first member may "prompt" or call forth the second. Thus, the role of rhyme shoud not be understood as deforming ready-made vocal complexes, but as deforming the *direction* of speech.

Habitual associations receive a particular significance here. In certain epochs of exact rhymes, they become not only a fact of poetry, but also of the poetic plot.

This reminds one of Boileau (Satire II):

> *Si je veux d'un galant dépeindre la figure,*
> *Ma plume pour rimer trouve L'abbé de Pure,*
> *Si je pense exprimer un auteur sans defaut,*
> *La raison dit Virgile, et la rime Quinault.*
> *Enfin, quoi que je fasse ou que je veuille faire,*
> *La bizarre toujours vient m'offrir le contraire.*
> *...Je ferois comme un autre; et sans chercher si loin,*
> *J'aurois toujours des mots pour les coudre au besoin.*
> *Si je louois Philis en miracles féconde,*
> *Je trouverois bientôt à nulle autre seconde;*
> *Si je voulouis vanter un object nonpareil,*
> *Je mettrois à l'instant, plus beau que le soleil.*

If I wish to depict a galant figure,
My pen for a rhyme hits upon the abbe of Pure,
If I want to show an author without fault,
The reason says Virgil, but the rhyme is Quinault.
In short, whatever I do or whatever I would make,
The bizarre always comes to offer me the opposite.
...I would like to do as others, and not going far,
Always find the words necessary to tack on.
If I praised Philis for prolific miracles,
I would soon find another just like her;
If I wished to praise an unparalleled object,
I would immediately come back with more beautiful than the sun.

(We note that this "prompting" of Boileau proceeds by means of similar principal signs of "words held in stock.")

Thus, the complaint about rhyme is a *plot of parody*, and at the same time a motivation for verbal constructions not connected by principal signs. ("Select a rhyme for a rhyme"—Goethe.) Vyazemsky, Zhukovsky, and Pushkin also used this.

Here is an example from Zhukovsky:

> .... *poteriannykh plotkov*
> *Nikak ne mozhet tam lovit' spina del'fina.*
> *I v samom dele eto tak.*
> *No znaite, nash del'fin ne del'fin-bashmak*
> *Tot samyi, chto v Moskve grafinia Katerina (pour la rime)*
> *Petrovna vzdumala tak vazhno utopit'...*
> ("Platok gr. Samoilovoi," 1819)

> .... lost kerchiefs
> Cannot be caught by the back of a dolphin.
> And this is actually so.
> But you know, our dolphin is not quite a dolphin—but a shoe
> That very same, which in Moscow countess Katerina (pour la rime)
> Petrovna thought so important to destroy...
> ("The Kerchief of Countess Samoilova")

The deliberately clumsy enjambment "Katerina/Petrovna" emphasizes the device here.

Thus, there is a type of play on rhymed connections here, which moves in two directions—the progressive and the regressive. "Katerina" (a comic *rejet*) is an example of a progressive connection with the word "del'fina" ("of a dolphin"). (We have the humorous remark of the author—"pour la rime.") But the second member of the rhyme "bashmak" ("shoe") was able to call up an entire "empty" line: "I v samom dele eto tak" ("And this is actually so").

Other examples of play on coupled lines in Zhukovsky can be seen in "V Komitet" ("To the Committee") from 1819, and others. Here the rhyme acquired the comical coloring which was canonical for trifling epistles.

In 1821, Vyazemsky freely translated a satire of Boileau (III, p. 226-7):

> Um govorit odno, a vzdorshchitsa svoe.
> Khochu l' skazat', k komu byl Feb iz russkikh laskov,
> Derzhavin rvetsia v stix, a popadet Kheraskov. [101]

The intellect speaks one way, but the fool another.
Were I to say to whom of the Russians the caress of Phoebus,
Derzhavin bursts into verse, but Khersakov arrives.

He himself used a more successful "plot of rhyme" in the poem "From Moscow ("Iz Moskvy) (1821, III, p. 253-4):

> Blagodariu vas za pis'mo —
> Uma liubeznogo triumo,
> O vy, kotoraia izdavna
> Ekaterina Nikolavna,
> Po russki prosto govoria,
> A na grammatiku smotria,
> Tak Nikolaevna—no chto zhe:
> Ved' russkii stikh, izbavi bozhe!
> Kakoi postrel, kakaia shal',
> Ved' russkii stikh ne graf Laval'...
> ...Komu kormilets Apollon,
> Tremia pomnozhennyi Anton,
> Da na zakusku Prokopovich,
> Zdes' rifma mne Vasily L'vovich...
> ...No radi boga samogo,
> Skazhite, Pushkind'iavol chto-li?
> A zdes'pod rifmu mne Go'goli...

I thank you for your letter,—
Mirror of an amiable mind,
O you, who for a long time have been
Ekaterina Nikolavna,
Speaking simply in Russian,
But according to the grammar,
It is Nikolaevna—oh, well!
This is Russian verse, God save us!

Such roguery, such senselessness,
Russian verse is not count Laval...
...To the one whose breadwinner is Apollo,
Multiply Anton by three,
For an appetizer take Prokopovich,
Here my rhyme is Vasily Lvovich...
...But for the sake of God himself,
Tell me, is Pushkin a devil?
And here for a rhyme I'll take Gorgoli.

Here it is not the play itself with rhyme that is interesting, but rather *the unwinding of the lyric plot,* which simulates, as it were, the coupling of line with line.

Pushkin used habitual associations of rhyme in order to destroy them. Having given an habitual *rhyme*, he simultaneously detached it from the text and deprived it of motivation. This meant an interruption and change of material in the compositional plan, and it bared the form:

Chitatel' zhdet uzh rifmy rozy-
Na, na, voz' im ee skorei.

The reader already awaits a rhyme for *rose—*
Here, here—hurry up and take it.

In this regard, all three (Pushkin, Zhukovsky, and Vyazemsky), of course, only continued the play consecrated by the Karamzinians, who in turn continued the tradition of French "comic" and "light" verse of the eighteenth century *(bouts rimes).*

In France, this play with habitual associations of rhyme was perhaps called forth by the specific conditions of Alexandrian verse. But in Russia as well, the isolation of this "prompting role" of rhyme stood on solid ground.

Towards the very end of the eighteenth century, a cautious relationship toward rhyme begins in the camp of the *archaists.* On one hand, S. Shikhmatov-Shirinsky advances the demand for difficult rhyme, therefore rejecting verbal rhymes. On the other hand, S. Bobrov begins a struggle against rhyme. The latter, in the preface to *Xersonida*, which was written in blank verse, wrote:

There is no doubt that our language is quite liberal in the conveying of rhymes, just as Italian is, after which it (Russian) is recognized as being second among European languages, especially in pleasantness. But if there is any poet, however wise, who feels that great weight which, thanks to rhyme and to the extension of words, must always

123

lower or weaken the best thought and strongest picture, and rather than enlivening, destroys that picture, then that poet must agree with me that rhyme, serving as a challenge to the most beautiful sensations and most refined thoughts, almost always kills the soul of the work.[102]

Vyazemsky's imitation of Boileau also apparently was on solid theoretical ground. Later he wrote: "Pushkin did not like my verses. Later, however, he agreed with me."

He apparently had in mind the following section of Pushkin's "Thoughts on the Road" ("Mysli na doroge"):

I think that for the present we will turn to blank verse. There are too few rhymes in the Russian language. One calls forth another. "Plamen'" ("ardour") inevitably drags after itself "kamen', "("stone"). From behind "chuvstva"("feelings") without fail emerges "iskusstvo" ("art"). Who has not been pestered by "liubov' "("love") and "krov' "("blood"), "trudnoi" ("difficult") and "chudnoi" ("wonderful"), "vernoi" ("true") and "litsemernoi" ("hypocritical") and others?

We note that Pushkin, in contrast to Boileau, indicates coupled words with even *remote* principal signs. It is habitual connections which are at the heart of the matter here. The more remote the principal signs of the connected words are in such habitual groupings, the more the feature of habitualness is emphasized. The role of these habitual rhymes in language, where they promote not only the formation, but also the consolidation of verbal groups, is well known:

Rhyme often calls forth in assorted languages various, and even contradictory opinions. In one language it argues for that which it guards against in another. In Danish, all that is old, and therefore good, is said to be "gammelt og godt," for linguistic harmony did not allow the connection "nyt og godt." It is otherwise in France: "tout beau, tout nouveau."

Here is the type of example introduced by Nyrop. Faret, a modest member of the academy, became a drunkard in verse only because his name rhymed with cabaret, "Tiberius" with "Biberius," and "Ehestand" ("wedlock") with "Wehestand" ("grief"), etc. [103]

Habitualness lowers the progressive *strength* of rhyme. If the word "plamen' "*inevitably* drags after itself "kamen'," then the same inevitability significantly lowers the dynamic feature in rhyme. (The prohibition of rhymes with similar formal elements must be partially based on this.)[104]

From this point of view, the introduction and canonization of blank iambic pentameter in the twenties and the introduction of inexact rhyme present themselves as features which destroy the fixed and automatic flow of verse.

The progressive strength of rhyme suffers not only from the habitualness of the connection, but also from the *unusualness or rarity of the first member*. The first member of the rhyme is advanced *by its position*. Being advanced *by its very character* (if this is not recognized as a device), it receives an *independent significance*, holding attention on itself, and at the same time losing much of its own *progressive* action. Here we see the weak rhythmical side of many rich rhymes.

Thus, rhyme with a surplus of progressive action in the first member may even influence the semantic relationship in a particular way, combining the principal sign of the first member with the coloring of the second member ("the inevitable"). This combination may weaken the semantic strength of the first member. One may compare this with the fact that in rhymed and alliterated pairs of words in language, *the first word almost always loses its own principal sign:* "Hülle und Fülle," "Knall und Fall."[105]

Thus, with solid, rhymed connections, the first member is, for the most part, semantically deformed, and in it advance oscillating signs in connection with the second member. Meanwhile, the second member proves to be less affected semantically (and, accordingly, is less intensively advanced). With rhyme having the full strength of progressive action, the second rhymed member is isolated, which promotes all the more strongly the confrontation of both members (the regressive feature). The greater the distinction of both rhymed members, their principal signs, and their objective and formal parts, the more strongly this confrontation will deform the group.

Thus, if two words rhyme with one, the semantic effect of the confrontation of alien words is enriched by the fact that the quantity of these words in unequal. Here are the area of *punning rhymes* is revealed, one of the major conditions of which is exactness:

Garol'dom—so l'dom.

Like Harold—with ice.

Consider the rhyme of Minaev:

Oblast' rifm moia stikhiia,
I *legko pishu* stikhi ia,
Bez razdum ia, bez otsrochki,
Ia k stroke begu ot strochki.
Dazhe s finskim skalam burym
Obrashchaius's kalamburom.

The area of rhymes is my element,
And I easily write verses,

125

Without meditation, without delay,
I run from line to line,
Even if the phrase is a dark-brown Finnish cliff
I return with a pun.

Consider the mosaic rhymes of Mayakovsky, which are without a doubt of comic origin.

"Broken" rhymes, where one word (or a very compact group) is divided into two rhymes, presents a curious pendant toward mosaic rhymes.

Consider these rhymes of Druzhinin:[106]

> *Ia v burnoi iunosti moei*
> *Liubil devitsu Veru,*
> *No bolee lujbil ia Drei-*
> > *Maderu.*

> *Liubil ia Anneshek i Liz,*
> *Shatalsia v magaziny,*
> *No bolee liubil ia iz*
> > *Doliny.*

> *Est'u menia priiatel' Klein:*
> *On liubit korchit' grafa,*
> *A vypit' razve dast vam Vein-*
> > *de-Grafa.*

> *V zharu vostorga moego*
> *Chital ia takzhe Sterna,*
> *No bol'she vypival ia go-*
> > *Soterna.*

> *Karman moi stal kak resheto,*
> *Lishilsia ia profitu,*
> *No s goria vypival ia Shato-*
> > *Lafitu.*

> *Raz chut' menia ne dernul chort*
> *Proekhat'sia po Reinu*
> *No vypit' predpochel ia Port-*
> > *Veinu.*

> *No raz' 'ezzhaia po Rusi*
> *Ot Narvy do Altaia,*
> *Vsekh chashche ispival ia si-*
> > *voldaia.*

126

I in my stormy youth
Loved a girl Vera,
But more I loved Dry-
                    Madeira.

I loved Annushkas and Lizas,
I roamed in the stores,
But I loved more what came from
                    The Valley.

I have a friend Klein:
He loves to play the count,
But to drink he gives you Vein-
                    de-Grafa.

In the heat of my enthusiasm
I also read Sterne,
But above all I drank up Haut-
                    Sauterne.

My pocket became like a sieve,
I was deprived of profit,
But out of sorrow I drank up Chateau-
                    Lafitte.

The devil hardly pulled me
Travelling along the Rhine,
I preferred to drink Port
                    Wine.

But driving about Rus—
From the Narva to the Altais,
I quite often emptied the *si-*
                    voldaia.

    In the last stanza there occurs a type of rupture of a word into two parts, each of which is comprehended anew: "si" (Russian) = "si" (Spanish) (an effect prepared for by the foreign particles "drei," "Vein," "Port," and "Shato-"). Therefore, "voldaia" = "Valdaia."

    In the rhyme "Garol'dom—so I'dom" the important feature undoubtedly lies in the realization of the word "Garol'dom" as divisible:

Garo —l'dom, so l'dom.

127

The comic effect here is a result of a part of the word becoming "semasiologized" (although incompletely). This is also true of other examples:

>...*poroi upriam,*
>...*poroiu priam.*   (Eugene Onegin, VIII)

>...*at times stubborn,*
>...*at times direct.*

The following example is from Heine: "Theetisch — aes-thetisch." Again, the word "aesthetisch" is divisible: "aes-thetisch," and the "semasiolization" of the second part results in the comic effect.

This device in Mayakovsky is refined and reinforced by the accentual deformation of rhyming words. Rhymes deform stresses. Here we see their role in the isolation *of verbal groups* revealed on one hand, and the confrontation *of heterogeneous vocal elements,* on the other:

>*Glazami vzvila vvys' strelu.*
>*Ulybku uberi tvoiu.*
>*A serdtse rvetsia k vystrelu.*
>*A gorlo bredit britvoiu.*

>With eyes she released upwards an arrow.
>Guard your smile.
>The heart strains toward the shot.
>The throat is infatuated with the razor.

In the first line, the *group* "vvys strelu" ("upwards an arrow") is progressively advanced, almost pressed into one whole. At the same time, this group deforms the word "vystrelu" ("shot") with its accentual character, cutting its intonation into parts similar to the parts of the first member of the rhyme: "vvys' strelu" —"vys-strelu." This emphasizes the second part of the word, which in the given case is the material part.

Isolated and compressed in the same manner is the group "uberi tvoiu" ("guard your...") in the second line. It also deforms the word "britvoiu" ("with the razor") in the accentual relationship, cutting it into parts similar to the first member: "bri-tvoiu." This inevitably isolates the formal part of the word in this case.

This emphasizing of parts of a word disturbs the correlation between the material and formal elements (and thus complicates the principal sign with oscillating signs). It makes the word, as Mayakovsky himself once noted, "fantastic." (That is, it promotes the advancement of oscillating signs in the words.)

The comic effect in Druzhinin is achieved by the abrupt isolation of particles and auxiliary words, and by their being raised to the level of full equality with words. These particles are confronted, via rhyme, with words which are syntactico-semantically important.

Consider the following piece of Pushkin's:

> *Boites' vy Elizy-ovoi?*
> *Sprosila raz K*
> *Net, vozrazil NN surovoi,*
> *Boimsia my Elizy-ovoi,*
> *Kak vy boites' pauka...*

> Do you fear Eliza-ovaia?
> Once asked K
> No, objected NN severe,
> We fear Eliza-ovaia,
> As you fear a spider...

The comic effect is not only achieved by the fact that the *significance of words* is imparted to the signs "-ovoi," "K," and so on, as transferred from the custom of the prosaic novel. The comic effect is also achieved by the *confrontation* of these with the words whose *endings* are emphasized on account of this practice. Thus, a part of a word proves to be more advanced.

I have indicated the abrupt cases with the observance of the greatest quantity of conditions. But in an incomplete, undeveloped manner, these investigations are possible in cases which are more paled.

Before us is the *confrontation of words* (of groups), a result of which is that one of the rhymed members (by the habitualness of rhymed connections, the first, but in some cases, the second) may be deformed. The word or group is isolated. Thus, some part of the word may receive a greater semantic significance. A redistribution of the material and formal parts may occur in the word (in the presence of the punning rhyme).

A. Schlegel, in an essay on Alexandrian verse, states how much strength the feature of *confrontation* created by rhyme may have in verse. He places in connection the *play of antitheses* and the pairing of rhymes. Schlegel indicates that the antitheses were called forth and supported in French poetry *by the very system of Alexandrian verse.* [107]

The importance of the feature of confrontation and of making equal compels us to look upon rhyme as a particular rhythmical simile, with a partial alteration of the principal sign of the rhymed member, or with the advancement of oscillating signs within it. Its importance as a semantic lever of incredible strength is beyond doubt.

129

And so, the constructive role of rhythm is revealed not so much in the obscuring of the semantic feature, as in its sharp deformation. To a large degree, this decides the question about the theory of the image (Potebnia). The internal contradiction at the basis of this theory, which takes one of the secondary phenomena of poetry as its constructive factor, was revealed in a polemic of Viktor Shklovsky. Without entering into the essentials of the discussion of this question here, I will only make several remarks.

In a passage from Quintillian quoted by Potebnia, we see an indication as to the diverse functions of the image:

> *Transfertur ergo nomen aut verbum ex eo loco, in quo proprium est, in eum, in quo aut proprium deest, aut translatum proprio melius est. Id facimus, aut quia necesse est, au quia significantius est, aut quia decentius.*[108]

And so, the noun or verb is taken away from that place in which it is proper, and transferred to a place where it should properly be absent, or at least transferred to a more appropriate place. We do this either out of necessity, or because of expressiveness, or because it is more beautiful.

It is characteristic that Potebnia does not emphasize in italics "translatum proprio melius est" ("transferred to a more appropriate place") (which would have been natural), but "proprium deest" ("it should properly be absent"). Out of the three functions of the image, he emphasizes the function "necesse est" ("out of necessity"). Thus, even here we collide with the prerequisite of the communicative nature of poetry at the basis of this theory, and with its ignoring of construction and structure.

However, if the image is not the constructive factor of poetry, this raises the question of its functional connections with it.

A. Rosenstein attempted to explain the image from the point of view of its emotional role. The poet chooses:

> ...that which has the greatest emotional significance for us, where he has several words for the presentation of the same idea. Thus, compelled by style (*Diction*), he says "steed" instead of "horse," "grove" instead of "woods," "bark" instead of "boat," "gold" instead of "money," "youth" instead of "young man," "elder" instead of "old man," etc. Having used these expressions in ordinary conversation, we call forth a reverse action. One cannot recognize many of these so-called selected (noble) words. They therefore receive a great emotional significance since *they do not have the characteristic definiteness*

130

of concept which is inherent in ordinary words. "[109]

Here the assertion on the "indefiniteness of meaning" in the image deserves attention. We should examine this concept that the image is an alienation from objectivity. (This was later developed by T. Meyer in his book *Stilgesetz der Poesie*.) In this point, one may cut out the connection of the image with verse, for it does not lie in the place of emotions. (Emotion is linked with objectivity in the same way it is linked with "indefiniteness."

The word in poetry, appearing simultaneously as a member of two series, is *successive*. The "unwinding of the material" (the terminology of V. Shklovsky) in poetry therefore also proceeds *via a successive path*. It is precisely here that the image, with its alienation from objectivity, its origin lying in the advancement of oscillating signs at the expense of the principal sign, and its feature of semantic *complication*, appears as a specific form of the unwinding of verse material. (Here I agree with R. Jakobson in his definition of the poetic image as a means of introducing new words. I also agree with V.M. Zhirmunsky's definition of the word in verse as the "theme.")[110]

This is why the image in verse and the prosaic image are not one and the same. In prose, where the development of the plot proceeds by different means, the function of the image is also different. Consider Pushkin: "Prose demands thought and more thought; brilliant expressions do not serve it. Verse is another matter."

The distinction of the prosaic and poetic genres is based on the successiveness of verse speech and on its dynamization. I have already mentioned that what is sensed as a fragment in a prosaic series will not be fragmentary in poetry. In general, the abyss between the prosaic and poetic genres is clear. (Attempts to draw them closer together only deepen this distinction.) *The laws of the development of plot in verse are different than in prose.*

This is based, by the way, on the distinction between *verse time and prosaic time.* In prose (owing to the simultaneity of speech) time is tangible. These, of course, are not real, temporal correlations between events, but rather relative ones. Nevertheless, Gogol's slowed-down story about the barber Ivan Iakovlevich eating bread with onions calls forth a comic effect because too much time (literary time) is spared to it.

In verse, time is quite intangible.

Trifles of the plot and large plot unites are made equal to each other by the general verse construction.

The perspective of verse refracts the plotting perspective.

This is the meaning of the constructive factor.

Therefore, dynamic form unwinds in the complex interaction of the constructive factor with that which is subordinated to it. The constructive factor deforms that which is subordinated to it. This is why it is useless to return to the investigation of the abstraction of the "word," existing in the consciousness of the poet and connected associatively with other words. Even these associative connections proceed not from the "word," but are directed *by the general dynamics of the structure.*

I am reminded once again of Goethe:

Significant effects depend upon various poetic forms. If the content of my *Roman Elegies* was set in the tone and meter of Byron's *Don Juan*, then it would prove to be quite suggestive."[111]

APPENDICES

When Tynianov entered Opoiaz, I was already in Prague, and we did not manage to see each other for a long time. However, the closeness of our "philological steps," our scientific quests, and our approaches clearly demanded a personal meeting. We first exchanged letters in the fall of 1928, when Yuri Nikolaevich underwent treatment in Berlin for assaults of sclerosis, a cruel ailment which would bring an end to his short life fifteen years later. Tynianov promised to stay with us in Prague. His letters to me, together with all my archives, were destroyed in March of 1939 when Hitler invaded Czechoslovakia. Miraculously, a bundle of letters of N.S. Trubeckoy* remained intact, along with type-written copies of several of my letters to him. On the 27th of October, I informed Nikolai Sergeevich about the coming arrival of Yu. N Tynianov and Grigori Osipovich Vinokur, who was travelling about Germany at that time. I invitedTrubeckoy, who often called on us from Vienna, to visit Prague again so that we might all see each other: "It would be so good if you could manage to come. There is so much to talk about. Tynianov will bring us all the news, and tell us how the members of Opoiaz are doing. And Vinokur is full of the problems of the Shpetian[1] or, as the Petersburgians call it, the 'special'[2] tendency. Do come. If it is possible, then bring with you the lecture on systems of vocalism."

In the beginning of November, Vinokur came for several days. He read the ninth lecture in the Prague Linguistic Circle, entitled "Linguistics and Philology." Meanwhile, Tynianov's treatment in Berlin was unexpectedly delayed throughout all of November and into the beginning of December. Of his two promised lectures—one on literary evolution, and one on extra—literary series in literature—only the first took place. It was read in the Circle on December 16, and was entitled "The Problem of Literary Evolution." The article retold and developed the contents of an article of Tynianov's from 1927, and gave rise to a lively exchange of opinions with the foremost Czech literary scholar of that time, Jan Mukaŕovský.

Trubeckoy came to the lecture of Tynianov, and Tynianov in turn was present at the December 18th lecture of Nikolai Sergeevich. This lecture was "The Comparison of Vocal Systems," the first, and perhaps the most penetrating of Trubeckoy's experiments in the area of comparative phonological analysis in the search for universal phonetic laws. This found its way, after being re-worked, into the first volume of *Works* of the Prague Linguistic Circle (1929). In order to acquaint Tynianov with our newest linguistic quests, we sent him to lectures in phonology. We had Trubeckoy, on one hand, and the chairman of the Circle, Vilem Mathesius, on the other, who submitted the English system of phonemes to analysis on December 14. On February 2nd, 1929, I wrote Trubeckoy that Tynianov had remained in Prague until the beginning of January: "It is a pity that you saw him when he was quite unstrung, for he recovered later on. He has such strength of thought and broad taste."

Against the background of the deep and clinging grief of a "blackamoor," as we called him in jest, in Yuri there gushed a clear spring of full-blooded humor and a gift of mischevious mockery. He was a master at improvising his own sparkling parodies, and at revealing the hidden parodies in classics read by him. With his shy, uneasy estrangement and reticence, and occasional unsociable quality was combined an unusual ability and readiness "to break through the wall." He accustomed himself to the spiritual constitution of all that was dear to him, both in the surrounding world and in poetry, which he "loved most of all." Perhaps the fundamental, innermost essence of all the historico-literary searches and historical novels and stories of Tynianov was his ingenuous spontaneous belief in the inseparable co-presence of the present and the past.

*See *N. S. Trubeckoy's Letters and Notes*, The Hague-Paris, 1975.

135

In other words, he believed in the unity of present memories and past prototypes and precursors.

Shortly before this, Tynianov had completed *The Death of Vazir Mukhtar (Smert' Vazir-Muxtara)*, and read us separate chapters and episodes with enthusiasm and genuine scenic artistry. He commented animatedly at those places which seemed most success- ful to him. For example, I am reminded of his masterful presentation and interpretation of the meeting of Griboedov and Lenochka Bulgarina, and a Caucasian prologue to the Persian mission of Vazir-Mukhtar. Here we see the dramatically lazy cue—"Destroy!"— of Aleksandr Sergeevich Griboedov to Ivan Grigorevich Burtsov, the fleeting dialogue of the master and the servant about the well-planned return home, and the last walk of "Griboed" among the sacks of straw. I remember how the author reproached himself in passing while reading for whatever was ill-planned in the process of creation. He especially reproached himself for his inattention regarding the resemblance of the sur- names of Aleksandr Griboedov and his servant Aleksandr Gribov, which prompted the probable conjecture that the latter was related to the former not only as a foster-brother, but as a blood brother as well. Tynianov returned to these details in an article in 1930, "How We Write."

The first volume of the works of Khlebnikov with an introductory article by Tynianov, which had just arrived from Moscow, provoked quite a few conversations. We both rejoiced that after countless burdensome delays, one experiment in publishing the collected works of the most significant Russian poet of our era, although far from perfection, had at last come out. The verbal insights of the Futurist Khlebnikov fever- ishly fascinated Yuri Tynianov. He was convinced by the story of how in 1919, the segment "ulitsy ulei" ("the hive of the street"), a manuscript of Khlebnikov's, lay on my desk, and was accidentally read by Mayakovsky. It promped him to suddenly ex- claim: "If only I could write like Vitya!" I am reminded of the brusque remark of Yu. N. on the separate disparities in our treatment of poetry, which was connected, in his words, with the fact that he was much older than myself when he at last came to the verses of Khlebnikov and associates, after being held in captivity by the artistic currents of the recent past.

Our scientific work, its results, our future tasks and broader perspectives were the major theme of long and heated conversations between us. Both books of Tynianov were the starting point here. The first of these was *Verse Semantics (Stikhovaya sem- antika)*, which, according to the author, was renamed *The Problem of Verse Language (Problema stikhotvornogo iazyka)* (1924) against his will by the publisher. The second of these, which was about to be published, was the volume of articles *Archaists-Inno- vators (Arkhaisty-novatory)*, which in turn acquired the strange and colorless title of *Archaists and Innovators (Arkhaisty i novatory)*. In spite of his artistic achievements and successes, Yu.N. categorically insisted upon critical literary investigations being his vital vocation. This is what he said to me at the end of 1928, but ten years later, at the end of a draft of his autobiography, Tynianov summed up: "I gave up being an his- torian of literature, and became a writer of fiction." The preferable consideration of "our reader," according to the author's assertion, "subsequently decided." But even in his dying days, when unconsciousness was interrupted and recognition returned, "he began to talk about theory of verse and theory of literature," according to the witness of a friend.

In his Prague reflections, Tynianov openly and correctly took into account all the factors of the deep crisis experienced by Opoiaz, and reflected in general on the status of the Russian science of literature. He clearly identified and revealed with merciless severity the internal symptoms of stagnation and decay, besides pointing to the intensified threats of a further aggravation of obstacles from without. It became clearer and clearer that with all its novelty and value of individual creative outbursts, the total landslide of Opoiaz, that is, the growth of separate, mechanistic operations with the notorious "sum of devices," prevented the necessary regeneration of formal analysis into a valuable, structural envelopment of language and literature. The substitution of this transition by a dead and academic inventory of forms, or by capitulatory attempts at a compromise with vulgar sociologism is unacceptable.

Sharing the views of Yu.N., I suggested renovating Opoiaz by means of a joint ideological work which would advocate the organic development of our science into a universal, radical revision of pan-scientific methodology. There arose the thought about joint theses. As an example of an effective declaration of future investigative tasks, the recent phonological proposals worked out by myself for the First International Linguistic Congress, and supported by N.S. Trubeckoy and S.I. Kartsevsky, served quite well. These were first approved by the Prague Linguistic Circle (14.II.1928), and then by the above-mentioned congress (The Hague, April of that year). In general, the form of joint principled statements seemed to us most suitable for the broad preparation of a systematic, scientific reconstruction. At the same time that I was working with Tynianov, I began to work with Petr Grigorevich Bogatyrev on some debatable theses on folklore as a special form of creation.

Tynianov and I, as I wrote Trubeckoy, "decided to restore Opoiaz, and in general to begin the struggle against inclinations such as Eikhenbaum's, not to speak of the eclecticism of Zhirmunsky's group, etc. We sketched out the theses together, wishing to propose a new Opoyaz as the basis of the declaration, or at least as an initial point of debate. I am sending you a specimen. Return with an opinion." Trubeckoy answered that he "was in general agreement" with the critical manifesto which was sent him.

The text of the "manifesto" was prepared in the middle of December by Tynianov and myself. In the approach to language, as well as to literature, it was a fruit of collective labor, so that it is simply not possible to answer the question which is repeatedly asked of me: where did the thought of one co-author end, and that of the other one begin? Upon returning home, Yu.N. gave our manuscript to *Novy Lef*, and it appeared in the twelfth number of that journal for 1928 (actually in the beginning of 1929). The editors placed an accompanying note with it: "Theses on the Contemporary Study of Language and Literature, Proposed by Roman Jakobson and Yuri Tynianov."

I will reproduce these theses here, which were published under the title of "problems of the Study of Literature and Language," and which were forgotten for quite a while. But in recent times, they have come out in translation in ten foreign languages, and have been subjected to animated analysis in the international scientific press.

1. Immediate problems of the Russian science of literature and language demand the clarity of a theoretical platform and decisive disassociation from more frequent mechanical pastings-together of a new methodology with old and outlived methods. It also demands a disassociation from the contraband presentation of naive psychologism and other second-hand methodologies in the guise of new terminology.

A disassociation from academic eclecticism (Zhirmunsky and others) and from scholastic "formalism," which substitutes terminology and cataloguing of phenomena for analysis, is necessary. A disassociation from the repeated transformation of systematic literary and linguistic science into episodic and anecdotal genres is necessary.

2. The history of literature (of art), being involved with other historical series, is characterized, as is each one of these other series, as a complex composite of specific structural laws. Without an elucidation of these laws, a scientific establishment of the correlation between the scientific series and other historical series is impossible.

3. The evolution of literature cannot be understood so long as the evolutionary problem is screened by questions of episodic, non-systematic genesis, whether this be literary (such as the area of literary influences), or extra-literary. Whether that which

137

is utilized in literature is literary or extra-literary material, it may only be introduced into the sphere of scientific investigation when it is examined from the functional point of view.

4. The sharp opposition between a synchronic (static) and a diachronic cross-section has recently been a fruitful working hypothesis, both for linguistics and for the history of literature, so long as it has indicated the systematic character of language (or literature) at each separate moment of its life. In its present state of achievement, the synchronic concept compels us to again re-examine principles of diachrony. As the concept of the mechanical agglomeration of phenomena was replaced by the concept of system and structure in the area of synchronic science, a corresponding replacement was made in the area of diachronic science. The history of a system is in turn a system. Pure synchronism now proves to be an illusion. Each synchronic system has its own past and future as inseparable structural elements of the system (a: archaism as a stylistic fact; a linguistic and literary background which is recognized as an out-lived, old-fashioned style; b: innovational tendencies in language and in literature, recognized as the innovation of the system).

The opposition of synchrony and diachrony was an opposition of the concept of system to the concept of evolution. This loses its principled importance so long as we admit that each system without fail is given as an evolution, and, on the other hand, that evolution inevitably carries a systematic character.

5. The concept of a literary synchronic system does not coincide with the concept of the naively-conceived chronological epoch. Not only works of art which are chronologically near each other enter into its composition, but also works which are drawn into the orbit of the system from foreign literatures and older epochs. The indifferent cataloguing of co-existent phenomena is insufficient, for it is their hierarchical significance which is important for a given epoch.

6. The assertion of the distinct concepts of "parole" and "langue" and the analysis of the correlation between them (the Geneva School) were extremely fruitful for the science of language. The problem of the correlation between these two categories (the present norm and the individual utterance) in literature as well should be submitted to a principled elaboration. Here the individual utterance cannot be examined irrespective of the existing complex of norms. (The investigator, disengaging the first from the second, inevitably deforms the examined system of artistic values, and destroys the possibility of establishing its immanent laws.)

7. The analysis of the structural laws of language and literature and of their evolution inevitably leads to the establishment of a restricted series of actually given structural types (or types of evolution of structures).

8. The revealing of immanent laws of the history of literature (and of language) allows us to characterize each concrete alteration of literary (and linguistic) systems. It does not allow us to explain the tempo of evolution or the choice of a path of evolution in the presence of several theoretically possible evolutionary paths. The immanent laws of literary (and linguistic) evolution present only an indefinite direction, which limits the possibilities to a certain quantity of decisions, but does not obligatorily create a unified decision. The question of the concrete choice of a path, or at least of the dominant, may be decided by means of analysis of the correlation of the literary series with other historical series. This correlation (a system of systems) has its own structural laws, which must be subjected to investigation. The examination of the correlation of systems without an account of the immanent laws of each system would be methodologically fatal.

9. Proceeding from the importance of further collective working out of the above-mentioned theoretical problems and concrete tasks, and flowing from these principles (the history of Russian literature, the history of the Russian language, the

138

typology of linguistic and literary structure, etc.), the renewal of Opoiaz under the chairmanship of Viktor Shklovsky is necessary.

Tynianov valued our scientific beliefs as a creed, but remained full of deep doubt as to its concrete results, the revival of Opoiaz, and the feasibility of further theoretico-scientific examinations in the given conditions. Besides this, he refused to believe in the immediate future of his own critical labors, and, as Lidiya Ginzburg noted in her reminiscences of Tynianov[3], "they did not reprint in the 1920s as they do in the sixties." Having conducted the guests home, I wrote to Trubeckoy: "By the way, because of Tynianov's and your equally bleak pessimism, and because of news which is more and more sad, I am suffering from such marasmus as I have never felt before. I work with great labor. This must be overcome." The volume of *Archaists and Innovators (Arkhaisty i novatory)* which was sent to me carried the inscription "To Roman Jakobson. without whom there is no Opoiaz/with great/friendship/Yu. Tynianov/1929.II.20." In reading it, I was reminded of the hymn of Opoiaz, which was read to me by Yuri and which he collaborated in composing. In it, melancholy alternated with joking. In the passage about me, the words "vzyvaem gromko" ("we blast loudly") rhymed with the question—"Kogda pridesh ty, Romka?" ("When are you coming, Romka?"). It is strange that later on, these lines found themselves being sung in some remote corner and were ascribed to Mayakovsky, apparently by association, since the same reduction of names is seen is his "Tovarishch Nette." From the efforts to resurrect Opoiaz, as Yuri Tynianov wrote me in 1929, nothing resulted. The consequences were preserved in his comic epistle to Pushkin:

> *Byl u vas*
> *Arzamas,*
> *Byl u nas*
> *Opoyaz*
> *I literatura.*
> *Est'"zakaz"*
> > *Kass,*
> *Est' "ukaz"*
> > *Mass,*
> *Est'u nas*
> *Mladshii klass*
> *I makulatura.*
> *Tam i tut*
> *Institut*
> *I gulit,*[4]
> *I glavlit*[5]
> *I otdel kulturnyi,*
> *No glavit*
> > *Bdit*
> *I agit*
> > *Sbit;*
> *Eto zhe vse byt,*
> *Byt literaturnyi.*

> You had
> Arzamas,
> We had
> Opoyaz
> And literature.

139

There is the "order"
       Of Cashboxes,
There is the "edict"
       Of the Masses,
We have
The youngest class
And pulp literature.
There and here
Is the institute
And gublit,
And glavlit,
And the cultural department,
But glavlit
       Keeps watch
And agit
       Churns;
This is everyday existence,
Everyday literary existence.

When Tynianov left Prague in the beginning of 1929, he stood in the carriage, and we, his friends, crowded below on the platform. Departure was announced, farewell salutations and wishes were exhausted, but the engine still did not move. A repertoire of appropriate jokes was set in motion, a clumsy silence ensued, and at last the train moved. But a minute later it returned to its former place in reverse motion, and this was repeated three times. Sliding the window open, the Tynianov concerned with film uttered: "It cannot perform the final scene." The locomotive suddenly started off obediently. In 1936, Yu.N., attempting for the last time to find a magician-doctor, went to Paris and sent us a telegram. He urged us to meet him in his train on his way through Czechoslovakia. But the railway timetable was mistaken in some way, and we never managed to see each other again.

1. *Gustav Gustavovich Shpet, Russian philologist and aesthetician (1878-1940).*
2. *Prof. Jakobson coins the adjective "shpetial'nyi" here, which is a punning combination of Shpet's name and the adjective "shpetsial'nyi", "special"), which was used quite frequently by the Moscow Linguistic Circle.*
3. *See Yuri Tynianov, pisatel'i uchenyi:vospominania razmyshlenia, vstrechi (Moskva, 1966).*
4. *"Gubernskii otdel literatury i izdatel'stv" ("Provincial Department of Literature and Publications").*
5. *"Glavnoe upravlenie po delam literatury i izdatel'stva" ("Chief Administration for Literary Affairs and Publishing"). This is the censorship board.*

1. *Dostoevskii i Gogol' (k teorii parodii)* — (Peterburg, 1921)
2. "Stikhovye formy Nekrasova" — (*Letopis' Doma Literatorov*, 1921, no. 14)
3. "Blok i Geine" — (*Ob Aleskandre Bloke. Sbornik statei*, Peterburg 1921)
4. "O kompozitsii 'Evgeniia Onegina.' " — (1921-22; first complete publication in 1975)
5. "Zapiski o zapadnoi literature" — (*Knizhnyi ugol*, 1921, no. 7—1922, no. 8)
6. "Tiutchev i Geine" — (*Kniga i revoliutsiia*, 1922, no 4)
7. "Serapionovy brat'ia," Al'manakh I — (*Kniga i revoliutsiia*, 1922, no.6)
8. "Oda ego siiatel'stvu grafu Khvostovu" — (*Pushkinist*, vol. IV, Moskva 1922)
9. "Mnimyi Pushkin" — (1922; unpublished until 1977)
10. "Georgii Maslov" — (1922 — introduction to Maslov *poema*)
11. "Molodoi Tiutchev" — (*Tiutchevskii sbornik (1873-1923)*, Petrograd 1923)
12. "Vopros o Tiutcheve" — (*Kniga i revoliutsiia*, 1923, no. 3)
13. "Illiustratsii" — (*Kniga i revoliutsiia*, 1923, no. 4)
14. "Literaturnyi al'manakh, I" — (*Kniga i revoliutsiia*, 1923, no. 4)
15. "Literaturnaia mysl'. Al'manakh II" — (*Pechat'i revoliutsiia*, 1923, no. 3)
16. "T. Rainov, *A.A. Potebnia*" — (*Russkii sovremennik*, 1924, no.1)
17. "Kino — slovo — muzyka" — (*Zhizn' iskusstva*, 1924, no. 1)
18. *Problema stikhotvornogo iazyka* — (Leningrad 1924)
19. "Slovar' Lenina-polemista" — (*Lef*, 1924, no. 1)
20. "Literaturnyi fakt" — (*Lef*, 1924, no. 2)
21. "Literaturnoe segodnia" — (*Russkii sovremennik*, 1924, no.1)
22. "Promezhutok" — (*Russkii sovremennik*, 1924, no. 4)
23. "Sokrashchenie shtatov" — (*Zhizn' iskusstva*, 1924, no. 6)
24. " 'Izvozchik' Nekrasova" — (*Zhizn' iskusstva*, 1924, no. 7)
25. "Zhurnal, kritik, chitatel' i pisatel' " — (*Zhizn' iskusstva*, 1924, no. 22)
26. "O stsenarii" — (*Kino*, Leningrad 1926, March 2, no. 9)
27. "O siuzhete i fabule v kino" — (*Kino*, Leningrad 1926)
28. "Arkhaisty i Pushkin" — (*Pushkin v mirovoi lit.*, Leningrad, 1926)
29. "Valerii Briusov" — (*Atenei. Istoriko-lit. vremennik*, Leningrad, 1926, no. 6)
30. "Pushkin i Tiutchev" — (*Poetika, I — Vremennik Otdela Slovesnykh Iskusstv Instituta Istorii Iskusstv*, Leningrad, 1926)
31. *Russkaia proza* — (*Sbornik statei pod red. B. Eikhenbauma i Yu. Tynianova*, Leningrad 1926)
32. "Oda kak oratorskii zhanr" — (Poetika — III)
33. "O literaturnoi evoliutsii" — (*Na literaturnom postu*, 1927, no.10)
34. "Disput o formal'nom metode" — (*Novyi lef*, 1927, no. 4)
35. "Ob osnovakh kino" — (*Poetika kino*, Leningrad 1927)
36. "Ot redaktsii" — (*Fel'eton. Sbornik statei*, Leningrad 1927)

37. *Russkaia poeziia XIX veka —Sbornik statei*   (introduction by Tynianov, Leningrad 1927)

38. "O Khlebnikove"   (Khlebnikov, *Sobranie proizvedenii*, edited by Tynianov and Stepanov, Leningrad 1928)

39. "Problemy izucheniia literatury i iazyka"   (*Novyi lef*, 1928, no. 12)

40. *Arkhaisty i novatory*   (Leningrad 1929)
    a. "Literaturnyi fakt"
    b. "O literaturnoi evoliutsii"
    c. "Oda kak oratorskii zhanr"
    d. "Arkhaisty i Pushkin"
    e. "Pushkin" (first time in print)
    f. " 'Argiviane,' niezdannaia tragediia Kiukhel'bekera"   (first time in print)
    g. "Pushkin i Tiutchev"
    h. "Vopros o Tiutcheve"
    i. "Tiutchev i Geine"
    j. "Stikhovye formy Nekrasova"
    k. *Dostoevskii i Gogol' (k terorii parodii)*
    l. "Slovar' Lenina-polemista"
    m. "Illustratsii"
    n. "Blok"   (altered version of "Blok i Geine")
    o. "Valerii Briusov"
    p. "Promezhutok"
    q. "O Khlebnikove"

41. V.K. Kiukhel'beker, *Dnevnik*   (preface by Tynianov, Leningrad 1929)

42. "O parodii"   (written 1929 — first published 1977)

43. "O Maiakovskom. Pamiati poeta"   (*Vladimir Maiakovskii*, single-issue newspaper, 1930, April 24)

44. "Epizod iz 'Puteshestviia v Arzrum' "   (*Zvezda*, 1930, no. 7)

45. "Kak my pishem"   (*Kak my pishem*, Leningrad 1930)

46. *Mnimaia poeziia*   (Leningrad 1931, intro. by Tynianov)

47. "Pushkin i Kiukhel'beker"   (*Literaturnoe nasledstvo*, 1934, no. 16-18)

48. "Zametki o litseiskikh stikhakh Pushkina"   (*Pushkin — Vremennik Pushkinskoi Komissii*, 1936, no. 1)

49. "O 'Puteshestvii v Arzrum' "   (*Pushkin — Vremennik Pushkinskoi Komissii*, 1936, no.2)

50. "Proza Pushkina"   (*Literaturnyi sovremennik*, 1937, no. 7)

51. "*Prokofii Liapunov* (tragediia Kiukhel'bekera)   (*Literaturnyi sovremennik*, 1938, no. 1)

52. "V.K. Kiukhel'beker"   (*Lit. sovremennik, 1938, no. 10*)

53. "Frantsuzkie otnosheniia V.K. Kiukhel'bekera"   (*Literaturnoe nasledstvo*, 1939, no. 33-34)

54. "Bezymennaia liubov' "   (*Literaturnyi kritik*, 1939, no. 5-6)

55. V.K. Kiukhel'beker, *Sochineniia*   (Leningrad 1939, ed. by Tynianov)

56. V.K. Kiukhel'beker, *Stikhotvoreniia*   (Moskva 1939, ed by Tynianov)

57. A. Akhmatova, *Iz shesti knig*   (Leningrad 1940, arranged by Tynianov)

58. "Zametki o Griboedove"   (*Zvezda*, 1941, no. 1)

59. "Kiukhel'beker o Lermontove" (*Lit. sovremennik*, 1941, no. 7-8)
60. "Suzhet 'Goria ot uma.' " (*Literaturnoe nasledstvo*, 1946, no. 47-48)

More Recent Editions of Tynianov's Criticism and Theory

Problema stikhotvornogo iazyka, stat'i (Sovetskii pisatel', M. 1965)
Arkhaisty i novatory (Wilhelm Fink Verlag, Munchen 1967)
Pushkin i ego sovremenniki (Nauka, Moskva 1969)
Poetika, istoriia literatury, kino (Nauka, Moskva 1977)

Fiction of Tynianov

Sobranie sochinenii v 2 tomakh (Goslitizdat, M.L., 1931)
tom I — *Kiukhlia*
tom II — *Smert' Vazir-Mukhtara*

Sochineniia (Goslitizdat, Leningrad 1941)
Kiukhlia, Podporuchik Kizhe,
Maloletnyi Vitushishnikov,
Voskovaia persona,
Pushkin: Detstvo

Izbrannye proizvedeniia (Goslitizdat, Moskva 1956)
Kiukhlia, Podporuchik Kizhe
Pushkin

Sochineniia v 3 tomakh (Goslitizdat, M.L., 1959)
tom I — *Avtobiografiia,*
Kiukhlia, Podporuchik Kizhe,
Voskovaia persona
Maloletnyi Vitushishnikov
tom 2 — *Smert' Vazir-Mukhtara,*
Chetyrnadtsatoe dekabria (a play)
tom 3 — *Pushkin*

More Recent Editions of Tynianov's Fiction

Izbrannoe (Izdatel'stvo literatura artistike, Kishinev, 1977)

Kiukhlia, Pushkin
Pushkin (Khudozhestvennaia literatura, Leningrad 1974)

Tynianov's Translations into Russian

G. Geine, "Satiry" (Academia, Leningrad 1927)
G. Geine, "Germaniia. Zimnaia skazka" (Goslitizdat, Leningrad 1933)
G. Geine, "Stikhotvoreniia" (Leningrad, 1934)

October 18, 1894	—	Yuri Tynianov born into family of doctor in Vitebsk province.
1904-1912	—	Tynianov studies in Pskov gymnasium.
1918	—	completes courses at St. Petersburg in Slavic and Russian studies.
1921	—	prints first critical work *Dostoevskii i Gogol'* in Opoyaz.
1924	—	prints article "Slovar' Lenina-Polemista" in journal *Lef* no. 1 (5).
1925	—	first historical novel published — *Kiukhlia.*
1926	—	The film "Shinel' " (combining elements of Gogol's "Shinel' " and "Nevskii prospekt") released, with script by Tynianov.
1926-1927	—	Tynianov writes series of articles on theory and practice of film.
1927	—	Historical novel *Smert' Vazir-Mukhtara* published in *Zvezda* (nos. 1,2,3,4,6,11,12 of 1927, nos. 1,2,4, 5,6 of 1928).
1927	—	*Podporuchik Kizhe* published in *Krasnaia nov'* no. 1.
1927	—	Tynianov's translation of H. Heine, "Satiry," printed in Leningrad.
1929	—	travels to Berlin and Prague.
1929	—	*Arkhaisty i novatory* published.
1930	—	writes *Voskovaia persona*, which is printed in 1932 in *Zvezda*, no. 1,2.
1932	—	begins work on *Pushkin*, a historical novel.
1933	—	*Maloletnyi Vitushishnikov* printed in *Literaturnyi sovremennik*, no. 7.
1933	—	Tynianov's translation of Heine published: "Germania. Zimniaia skazka."
1934	—	"Stikhotvoreniia," Tynianov's third translation of Heine, printed in Leningrad.
1934	—	*Poruchik Kizhe* released as film with script by Tynianov, based on his novel *Podporuchik Kizhe.*
1935-1937	—	First part of *Pushkin* printed in *Literaturnyi sovremennik*, nos. 1,2,3,4 of 1935, with title of *Detstvo.* Part 2 of *Pushkin*, entitled *Litsei,* published in nos. 10,11,12, of 1936, and nos. 1,2 of 1937.
1939	—	Tynianov awarded order of the Red Banner of Labor.
1941	—	Tynianov evacuated from Leningrad to Perm', where he continued work on *Pushkin.*
1943	—	part 3 of *Pushkin* published in *Znaniia*, nos. 7,8, under title of *Iunost'.*
1943	—	Tynianov dies in Moscow.

Arzamas, literary society of followers of Karamzin. Its members included Zhukovsky, Batiushkov, Vyazemsky, and Pushkin. The society initially was established in order to parody the conservative Shishkovites.

Batiushkov, Konstantin Nikolaevich (1787-1855). Russian poet, member of "Arzamas." Batiushkov suffered from severe mental illness from 1821 until his death.

Bely, Andrei, pseudonym of Boris Nikolaevich Bugaev (1880-1934). Symbolist.

Blok, Aleskandr Aleksandrovich (1880-1921). Russian Symbolist Poet.

Breal, Michel Jules (1832-1915). French linguist and philologist.

Bobrov, Semen Sergeevich (1760-1810). Russian poet.

Bryusov, Valery Iakovlevich (1873-1924). Russian Symbolist poet.

Burinsky, Z.A., Russian poet of the early nineteenth century.

Chekov, Anton Pavlovich (1860-1904). Russian playwright and short story writer.

Darmesteter, Arsene (1846-1888). French linguist, specialist in Romance languages.

Derzhavin, Gavrila Romanovich (1743-1816). Russian lyric poet.

Dmitriev, Ivan Ivanovich (1760-1837). Russian poet and satirist.

Druzhinin, Aleksandr Vasil'evich (1824-1864). Russian journalist, literary critic, and satirist.

Engel'gardt, Nikolai. Russian literary historian.

Erdmann, Benno (1851-1921). German philosopher and psychologist.

Fet, Ananasy Afanasevich (1820-1892). 19th century Russian poet.

Flechier, 17th century French man of letters and orator.

Gogol', Nikolai Vasil'evich (1809-1852). Russian novelist, short story writer, and playwright.

Gorky, Maksim, pseudonym of Aleksei Maksimovich Peshkov (1868-1936). Russian novelist, dramatist, and short story writer.

Grossman, Leonid Petrovich (1888-1965). Literary theoretician, Dostoevsky scholar and novelist.

Guyau, nineteenth century French poet and philosopher.

Heine, Heinrich (1797-1856). German poet and prose writer.

Iakubinsky, Lev Petrovich (1892-1945). Russian linguist and literary scholar.

Ivanov, Vsevolod Vyacheslavovich (1895-1963). Russian novelist, short story writer, and playwright.

Kahn, Gustave (1859-1936). French poet, also a theoretician of *vers libre*.

Karamzin, Nikolai Mikhailovich (1766-1826). Russian poet, novelist, and historian.

"Karamzinians," followers of Nikolai Mikhailovich Karamzin. The Karamzinians wished to get rid of heavy and ornate Church Slavicisms, and to replace these with lighter French terms and syntax. They advocated the use of the "middle style" in both verse and prose.

Kireevsky, I.V. (1806-1856). Slavophile, editor of several journals and literary reviews.

Kliuev, Nikolai Alekseevich (1887-1937). Russian poet.

Kostrov, Ermil Ivanovich (1750-1796). Russian poet and translator.

Khlebnikov, Velimir, pseudonym of Viktor Vladimirovich Khlebnikov (1885-1922). Russian Futurist poet.

Lermontov, Mikhail Iurevich (1814-1941). Russian poet, playwright and novelist.

Lomonosov, Mikhail Vasilevich (1711-1765). Russian scientist, poet, and theoretician of verse.

Madelung, Aage (1872-1949). Danish novelist. *The Man From the Circus (Zirkus Mensch)* was written in German.

Maikov, Apollon Nikolaevich (1821-1897). Nineteenth century Russian poet.

Marmontel, 18th century French writer of tales. Tynianov refers to his *Mémoires d'un père* (1804) (trans. B. Patmore, *Memoirs of Marmontel,* 1930), in which the author gives impressions of fellow French writers.

Martynov, Ivan Ivanovich (1771-1833). Russian translator.

Meyer, Theodor Alexander (1859-?). German aesthetician and literary historian.

Meumann, Ernst (1862-1915). German psychologist and aesthetician.

Mayakovsky, Vladimir Vladimirovich (1893-1930). Russian Futurist poet and playwright, committed suicide in 1930.

Minaev, Dmitry Dmitrievich (1835-1889). Minor Russian poet.

de Montesquiou, Robert (1855-1921). French poet.

Old Church Slavic, a South Slavic ecclesiastical and scholarly language.

Eugene Onegin, a novel in verse by Aleksandr Sergeevich Pushkin (1799-1837).

Nekrasov, Nikolai Alekseevich (1821-1878). Russian civic poet, journalist and publisher.

Nel'dikhen, Sergei Evgen'evich (1891-1942). Russian poet.

Novalis, pseudonym of Georg Friedrich Philipp, Freiherr von Hardenburg (1772-1801). German poet and theoretician of Romanticism.

Nyrop, Kristoffer (1858-1931). Danish philologist.

Paul, Hermann (1846-1921). German historical linguist and philologist.

Paul, Jean, pseudonym of Johann Paul Friedrich Richter (1763-1825). German novelist.

Petrov, V.P. (1736-1799). Russian poet and translator.

Pletnev, Petr Aleksandrovich (1792-1865). Russian poet and critic.

Polevoy, N.A. (1796-1846, Editor of the *Moscow Telegraph* from 1825-1834.

Polonsky, Iakov Petrovich (1819-1898). Minor poet of the nineteenth century.

Potebnia, Aleksandr Afanasevich (1835-1891). Russian and Ukrainian philologist, professor at Kharkov University.

Potemkin, Petr Petrovich (1886-1926). Russian poet and translator.

Pushkin, Aleksandr Sergeevich (1799-1837). Russian poet, prose writer, and dramatist. By common consent, Pushkin is considered to be the greatest master of the Russian language.

Quintilianus, Marcus Fabius (30/40 — c. 100 A.D.) Roman rhetorician and orator.

Raich, Semen Egorovich (1792-1855). Russian poet, literary critic, and translator.

Remizov, Aleksei Mikhailovich (1877-1957). Russian novelist and short story writer.

de Ronsard, Pierre (1524-1585). French poet and aesthetician.

Rosenstein, Alfred, German philologist.

Rozwadowski, Jan Michal (1867-1935). Polish linguist, professor at Krakow University.

Saran, Franz (1866-1931). German historian of literature.

Satirikon, Russian journal of satire. It appeared in St. Petersburg from 1908 until 1914, and was published by M.G. Kornfeld.

Shcherba, Lev Vladimirovich (1880-1944). Russian linguist, student of Baudouin de Courtenay.

Shengeli, Georgy Arkad'evich(1894-1956). Russian poet and translator.

Shevchenko, Taras Grigorevich (1814-1861). Ukrainian poet, playwright, painter, and nationalist. He wrote in both Ukrainian and Russian.

Shevyrev, Stepan Petrovich (1806-1864). Professor of Russian literature at Moscow University, literary historian, and poet.

Shirinsky-Shikhmatov, Prince S. (1783-1837). Russian poet.

Schlegel, August Wilhelm (1767-1845). German critic, theoretician of literature, and poet.

"Shishkovites," followers of Admiral Aleskandr Semenovich Shishkov (1753-1841). Shishkov opposed the westernization and modernization of Russian literature and the Russian literary language. Shishkovites advocated usage of Old Church Slavic, the high poetic style, and utilization of various aspects of old Russian literature.

Sievers, Eduard (1850-1932). German philologist and literary historian.

de Souza, Robert, late 19th century radical experimenter in free verse.

Sumarokov, Aleksandr Petrovich (1717-1777). Russian poet, playwright, and fable writer.

Tiknonov, Nikolai Semenovich (1896-). Russian poet.

Tyutchev, Fedor Ivanovich (1803-1873). Lyric and metaphysical poet of the nineteenth century.

Tolstoy, Count Aleksei Konstantinovich (1817-1875). Russian playwright and poet.

Tredyakovsky, Vasily Kirillovich (1703-1768). Russian poet, translator, and theoretician of prosody.

Turgenev, Aleksandr Ivanovich (1785-1846). Fellow-traveller of *Arzamas*.

Turgenev, Ivan Sergeevich (1818-1883). Russian novelist, poet, and playwright.

Uhland, Ludwig (1787-1862). German lyric poet, political activist.

Vyazemsky, Prince Peter Andreevich (1792-1878). Russian poet, journalist, co-founder of literary society known as *Arzamas*.

Viele-Griffin, Francis (1864-1937). French poet, theoretician of free verse.

Volkonsky, Sergei Mikhailovich (1860-1937). Russian critic and aesthetician.

Wölfflin, Heinrich (1864-1945). Swiss art historian and aesthetician.

Wundt, Wilhelm (1832-1920). German psychologist, physiologist, and philosopher.

Yakubinski, Lev Petrovich (1892-1945). Russian linguist and literary scholar.

Yazykov, Nikolai Mikhailovich (1803-2847). Russian poet of the nineteenth century.

Zhirmunsky, Viktor Maksimovich (1891-1971). Russian philologist and theoretician of verse.

Zhukovsky, Vasily Andreevich (1783-1852). Russian poet, translator, member of *Arzamas*.

1. In saying this, of course, I do not object to the "connections of literature with life." I only doubt the correctness of the formulation of the question. Is it possible to speak of "life and art" when art is also "life"? Is it necessary to still search for a special utility of "art" if we do not search for a utility of "life"? Another concern is originality and the inner regularity of art in comparison with actual existence, science, etc. How many misunderstandings have occurred with historians of culture as a result of their taking a "thing of art" as a "thing of actual existence"! How many historical "facts" are called to mind which upon verification turned out to be traditional, literary facts, and in which legend only substituted historical names! Where actual existence enters into literature, it also becomes literature, and must be evaluated as a literary fact. It is interesting to observe the significance of artistically-presented everyday life in an epoch of literary crises and revolutions, when the line of literature predominating and recognized everywhere is unraveling and exhausting itself, but another direction has not yet been found. In such periods, artistically-presented everyday life itself temporarily becomes literature, taking its place. When the high line of Lomonosov fell in the Karamzinian epoch, the trifles of literary domestic custom became a literary fact—correspondence of friends, a fleeting joke. But the whole point of this phenomenon is that the fact was raised to the power of a literary fact! In an epoch of the rule of high genres, this same domestic correspondence was only a fact of everyday existence, not having a direct relationship to literature.

2. *Razgovory Gete s Ekkermanom*, translation by Averkiev, I., p. 338-41. [J.P. Eckermann, *Conversations with Goethe*, trans. Girela C. O'Brien (New York: Ungar, 1964)]

3. Consider "The Nose" of Gogol, the essence of which is this play with equivalents of the hero. The nose of Major Kovalev is substituted by the "Nose," wandering along Nevskii Prospekt, etc. The "Nose" prepares to run away to Riga, but while getting into a mail coach, is captured by a policeman. Then he (!) is returned in a rag to his owner. What is remarkable in this grotesquery is not the equivalent of the hero, which is not interrupted for even a minute, or the equality of the nose with the "Nose." What is grotesque here is only the play on this double plane. The very principle of unity on which the effect is based is not violated, so that the reference to the grotesqueness of the work does not deprive the example of typicality. Goethe's examples, however, are not related to the area of the grotesque.

4. Often the sign itself or the very name is the most concrete feature of the hero. Consider the onomatopoetic surnames in Gogol. The concreteness which is called forth by the unusually articulated expressiveness of a name is quite strong, but the specificity of this concreteness is immediately revealed upon attempting to translate it into another specific concreteness. Illustrations in Gogol or reliefs on a monument to Gogol murder this Gogolian concreteness. This does not mean they cannot be concrete in and of themselves.

5. With the example of the history of the Russian octave, one can trace how in various epochs one and the same literary phenomenon fulfills various functions. In the 20's, the archaist Katenin advocated the octave as a stanza both important and necessary for large epic genres. In the 30's, the octave was not entrusted with a generic task, but rather a purely artistic one.

6. *The Moscow Observer (Moskovskii Nabliudatel',)* 1835, part III, p. 5-6.

7. "Letters of I.I. Dmitriev to Prince Viazemskii" ("Pis'ma I.I. Dmitrieva k.kn. Viazemskomu,") *Starina i Novizna*, book II, p. 163.

8. Barsukov, *Life and Works of Pogodin (Zhizn' i trudy Pogodina,)* III, p. 304-6.

9. Therefore, V. Shklovskii makes use of the concept of *motivation*, where there is a primary introduction into the plot of some motif in agreement with the rest.

10. Karamzin, Smirdin edition, vol. III, p. 528.

11. Consider S. Marin on Karamzin: "Let him call a service record a poem." *Conversation Society of Lovers of the Russian Word (Beseda Liubitelei Russkogo Slova,)* vol. III, p. 121. The exact word of the Karamzinians was a service record of its time, making itself felt for its exactness. The very smoothness of the word was a formal element, though a negative one. Still more characteristic is the remark about I.I. Dmitriev by one of the leading Karamzinians, P. Makarov: "In order to estimate our dear Poet's true worth, we must feel overcome by his attempt to conceal it under a shading of lightness. We must guess the places which under another pen would have been worse." [P. Makarov, second edition, 1817, vol. II, p. 74, *Works and Translations of I. Dmitriev (Sochinineiia i perevody I. Dmitrieva.)*] Only with the disappearance of these conditions, with the automatization of art, could this smoothness come into view as being self-evident, and could the thought arise that in this negative characteristic of the poetic word could be seen its positive characteristic.

12. See my article "Nekrasov's Verse Form" ("Stikhovaia forma Nekrasova,) *Letopis' Doma Literatorov,*1921, no. 4.

13. This last claim is important for it shows that even if Grammont's classic study, *French Verse, Its Means of Expression, and Its Harmony (Le vers francais, ses moyens d'expression, son harmonie)* seeks to elucidate the expressive function of verse, starting exclusively from motivated material, it leads to conclusions whose very essence is questionable.

These conclusions chiefly concern the illustrative role of rhythm and harmony. Rhythm and harmony are taken to be expressive means when they underscore the sense of the verse text, i.e., when they are motivated. However, here it is clear that the element of the expressiveness of rhythm completely coincides with the expressiveness of the text, so that it resists observation. Thus, in essence, what is investigated is not the question of the expressiveness of rhythm, but rather how much it is justified by the semantics (and even, perhaps, how much a definite semantics demands a definite rhythm, cf. the analysis of Hugo's ode "Napoleon I"). Taking the motivated as the *typical* case, Grammont considers it the *norm*. Therefore, he considers, for example, all modern *vers libre* as an error, since the changes in the rhythmical groups don't coincide with the semantic changes. It is natural under this view that verse rhythm is given functions beforehand which are inherent in general speech activity (emotionality and communicativeness).

14. See the article on this by B.M. Eikhenbaum in *Through Literature (Skvoz' literaturu)*; S.I. Bernshtein's "The Voice of Blok" ("Golos Bloka") (soon to appear).

15. Wundt, *Foundations of Physiological Psychology (Osnovy f. Psikhologii)*, vol. III, ch. XVI, p. 186.

16. Potebnia, *Notes on the Theory of Literature (Iz zametok po teorii slovesnosti)*, p. 107.

17. *Untersuchungen zur Psychologie und Aesthetik des Rhythmus*, Philos. Stud., Leipzig, Vol. X, p. 94.

18. Op. cit. p. 408. With us in Russia, both tendencies have spread, almost without residue between the reading of poets and the reading of actors. (See B.M. Eikhenbaum, "O chtenii stikhov.")

19. Fr. Saran, *Deutsche Verslehre*, Munchen, 07, VIII.

20. The segment is typical, since it presents an analogy with the beginning of stanzas VII and VIII-

Ty zhdal, ty zval...
You waited, you called...
O chem zhalet ...
Of what does he grieve...

This, together with the special systematic stanzaic distribution of phrases, prepares us somewhat for the fragmentary beginning of this stanza.

21. *Iz zametok po teorii slovestnosti*, p. 15. This is why an omission in prose is much less significant. In verse, an omission ("any text") has a metrical characteristic

which quantitatively colors it much more exactly, imparting to it a dynamic definiteness. In this sense, it acts in a much more definite direction than in prose. From this point of view, the startling experiment of the German futurist Kulka is interesting. A book of verse published in 1920 is limited to the graphic verse arrangement of punctuation marks, which gives the system of intonation a definite "verse" coloring.

Such were the experiments, it seems, done by V. Khlebnikov. However, one should note that even in prose the graphic may be refined in order to create the illusion of quantitative-syntactical ties. Consider Heine:

> ...*Der Satan, wenn er meine Seele*
> *verderben will, flüstert mir ins*
> *Ohr ein Lied von dieser ungewein-*
> *ten Thräne, ein fatales Lied mit*
> *einer noch fataleren Melodie, —ach,*
> *nur in der Holle hort man*
> *diese Melodie!—*.........
> ....
> .... (1843 edition)

22. Consider J.B. Rousseau, "L'ode aux princes Chretiens sur l'armement des Turcs," and others. Also consider the ode of Neledinskii-Meletskii, "On Time" ("Na Vremia"):

> *Prostranstvo smeriano Uranii rukoiu;*
> *No, vremia, ty dushoi ob' 'emelsh'sia odnoiu.*
> *Nezrimyi bystryi tok vekov i dnei i let,*
> *Dokol' eshche ne pal ia v zemnuiu utrobu,*
> *Vlekom toboi ko grobu,*
> *Derznu, ostanovias', vozzret' na tvoi polet.*

> Space is measured by Uranus' hand;
> But, time, you are contained by the soul alone.
> Invisible, quick current of centuries, and days and years,
> Since I have not yet fallen into the earthly womb,
> On the way with you to the grave,
> I will dare, halting, to gaze upon your flight.

23. See the account of Maiakovskii, collected in *Pushkin and his Contemporaries*, *(Pushkin i ego sovreminniki)*, 4th edition, p. 5, no. 14. Incidentally, P.O. Morozov falsely placed in the text of his publication (v. I, p. 345) the completely unfounded comment: "This stanza remained unwritten."

24. "Filling in" as if the lines were omitted is illegitimate, even if Pushkin had substituted his verses with the dots themselves. Such filling in arises from relating to the artistic creation as a keyhole behind which something is concealed.

25. Other examples of equivalents are stage directions in verse drama placed in the text, and stage directions of many Symbolists, not having the significance of scenic indications, but introduced as equivalents of action. (Consider *The Life of a Man* by Andreev.)

26. For the sake of convenience, I am considering here the extreme and consistent acoustic approach, dwelling upon the early work of Fr. Saran "Ueber Hartmann von Aue" (*Beitr. zur Gesch. d. deutsch. Sprache und Lit.*, vol. xxiii, 1898) for the typicality of its appraoch. Later, in *Deutsche Verslehre* (Munchen, 1907), the extremity of the acoustic approach is significantly concealed and is not nearly so clear.

Here in Russia, the broadening of the concept of rhythm was introduced by the work of B.V. Tomashevskii ("Problema stikhotvornogo ritma," *Lit. Mysl'*, 23, II).

27. See *Deutsche Verslehre*, p. 97: "Verschiedenheiten der Artikulation."

28. See his early work, p. 44. It is characteristic that in Saran's latest definition of rhythm, the word "acoustic" is discarded. *Deutsche Verslehre, p. 132.*

29. What is remarkable here is the thought (also introduced by Sievers in his *Rhytmisch-melodische Studien*) on the counteraction of the factors of rhythm against each other. If we remember that Saran introduces the "text" into the concept of rhythm, then verse here is confirmed as the dynamic interaction of a multitude of factors. It is interesting how in cases of metrical monotony Pushkin resorts to ornate rhyme and "instrumentation" as counteracting features. (Consider "Skazka o tsare Saltane.") It is also characteristic that in epochs of search for new rhythmical means, epochs of rhythmical disorder, there arises in poetry a recognition of the correlation of the many elements of verse. Thus, Semen Bobrov advocated the substitution of rhyme with the general euphony of verse:

> If one reads Pope himself in the original, one can feel his fine
> voice and shapeliness more in the skillful and regular arrange-
> ment of vowels and consonants in the very flow of speech than
> in rhymes, which are not employed for the general agreement of
> musical tones.

(S. Bobrov, *Khersonida*, 1804, p. 7) From this point of view, it is curious how rhyme is fused with the remaining factors of rhythm and enters into its system. Thus, in 1820 Kiukhel'beker distinguished three types of measures, of which

> ...the second, borrowed by Lomonosov from the Germans,
> is based on the stress of words or on feet, and on this accord
> in the end of verses, which we are in the habit of calling rhyme.
> The third is this same measure, but without rhyme, an imitation
> of the quantitative measure of the ancients."

(*Nevskii Zritel'*, 1820, part I, no. 2, p. 112, "Vzgliad na tekushchuiu slovenost' ") ("A Look at Current Literature").

30. V. Zhirmunskii, *The Composition of Lyric Verse* (*"Kompozitsiia liriceskikh stikhotvorenii"*), p. 90.

31. Wundt, *Völkerpsychologie*, vol. 3, p. 346 *[Folk Psychology]*

32. *Galateia*, 1830, no. 17, p. 20-31.

33. *A Pushkin Collection in Honor of S.A. Vengerov* (*Pushkin sbornik pamiati S.A. Vengerova*), 23, p. 329-354.

34. See "Rassuzhdenie ob ode," Grot edition, vol 7.

35. Bernshtein, p. 350. The graphic plays such a role, argues Rad. Koshutich (*Grammatika russkogo iazyka.*) Petrograd, 1919, p. 342).

> The graphics of forms such as 'pole,' 'more,' 'nashe,' 'zolotoe,' etc.,
> and of such forms as 'vol',' 'prostor',' 'chash',' and 'poko'' proved
> too attractive. Poets utilized them, equating the first forms with the
> second, phonetically as well, in comparison with the literary
> pronunciation. They are not pairs.

36. We recognize how much importance the syntactic factor has for rhyme by comparing the weakly sensed rhyme (3-4)-10 of the first stanza of the poem introduced with the rhyme of the second stanza:

1. *Kak nad bespokoinym gradom,*
2. *Nad dvortsami, nad domami,*
3. *Shumnym ulichnym dvizhen'em,*
4. *S tusklo rdianym osveshchen'em*
5. *I bezumnymi tolpami,*
6. *Kak nad etim dol'nym chadom*
7. *V chernom vysprennem predele,*
8. *Zvezdy chistye goreli,*
9. *Otvechaia smertnym vzgliadam*
10. *Neporochnymi luchami.*

1. Just over the troubled city,
2. Over the palaces, over the homes,
3. With noisy street traffic,
4. With dimly glowing lighting,
5. And with mad crowds,
6. Just over this earthly fume
7. In the black lofty bound
8. The pure stars burned,
9. Replying to the deathly glance
10. With immaculate rays.

The rhyme (2-5)-10 of the second stanza is much more perceptible than the rhyme (3-4)-10 of the first stanza. There is no doubt that several factors are at work here: 1.) the presence of an internal rhyme in the first rhymed member -"nad dvortsami, nad domami" ("over the palaces, over the homes"); 2.) the greater proximity of (2-5)-10 in the second stanza than (3-4)-10 in the first; 3.) the greater progressive strength in the second stanza of the first member (2) rhyming with the second member (5) across only two lines, whereas in the first stanza the rhyme is allowed in the very next line(3-4); 4.) the absence of the rhymed momentum AB-AB.

Nevertheless, we are scarcely mistaken if we relate the larger progressive strength of the rhyme not entirely to these factors, but to the same (and perhaps even larger) degree, to the distinction in the syntactic structure of the stanza. In the first place, this gives an even intonation of a narrative character (parataxis of narrative suggestions, arranged according to metrical rank). Secondly, it gives a strained intonation of a complex suggestion, in which the second rhymed member is located just on the border of an intonational alteration, in the same strained intonational area.

37. To a certain extent, of course, even the general phonic background may prepare for the special role of these or of other sounds, but this progressive role is extremely weak. Here, in the inequality of progressive and regressive features, and in the predominating role of the regressive is a complete distinction between the rhythmical functions of "instrumentation" and rhyme, which "euphony" threatened to unite into one concept. This very fact makes "instrumentation" as a factor of rhythm secondary in comparison with meter.

38. The indicated facts of equivalents, which contradict the acoustic approach to verse and to rhythm, do not contradict the motor-forces approach ("motorno-energeticheskii podkhod"). The objective sign of rhythm is the *dynamics* of vocal material, whether this is given in the shape of a system, or in the shape of orientation toward a system. Attempts to join the basis of rhythm with the temporal feature end in failure. Lotze stated the "paradox" that time does not play any role whatsoever in verse rhythm (Lotze, *Geschichte d. Aesth.*, p. 300). Experimental investigations lead to the complete negation of isochronism.* Where those pursuing a temporal system

see a pause (the concept of the "pauznik"), the latest investigators see a greater quantity of spent energy.** Regarding the impossibility of establishing isochronism, Rousselot wrote:

> For my own part, I suppose a major element of rhythm is in vowel sounds perceived by the ear, but I think, however, that this is not the sole basis for the poet. Would it not then follow to search for the source of rhythm in the organic feeling of the poet? He articulates (*articule*) his verses and speaks them to his own ear, which judges rhythm, but does not create it. And if the poet were mute, to him each sound would be represented as an expiratory effort, corresponding to the movement of organs, his production... From this, I conclude that rhythm is not based on acoustic time, but on time of articulation" (*Principes de phonétique expérimentale par l'abbé P.J. Rousselot, II, p. 307*).

If one cannot doubt the correctness of the formulation of the problem, we can doubt the correctness of its solution. "Articulatory time" is a palliative which does not resolve the significance of the absence of isochronism, but complicates the question even more. "Subjective time," of course, saves the position, but upon closer analysis proves to be a complex derivative, at the base of which lies a forceful feature—the feature of "expended work." Otherwise, the lines in *vers libre*, or, better yet, in the fable would not be sensed in an identical way as being competent. It is quite clear that a line consisting of one word and a line consisting of many long words, even taking into account the "subjectiveness" of time, must be unequal in value. Meanwhile, the whole point of these lines is that they are all equal in value as verses, in spite of their enormous temporal difference, for on each we spend (or should spend) a particular and even equivalent amount of work.

Not the acoustic concept of time, but the motor-forces concept of spent work should be placed at the center of the discussion of the question of rhythm.

Ordinary vocal classification places rhythmical speech in an unusual classification. The opinion of Wundt that verse rhythm is a type of emphasizing or condensation of the rhythm of conversational speech presents itself as unfounded. Rhythm of conversational speech is one of the factors of speech not made dynamic (resp. complex), and is unessential in itself for the communicative function. One can speak, perhaps, about the emphasis and condensation of the rhythm of conversational speech in a definite direction only upon analysis of the rhythm of artistic prose. Rhythm of the clause is one of the factors in verse of the dynamic system of rhythm, a system of interaction. Here especially it collides with metrical articulations. Verse rhythm appears as a result of many factors, one of which is vocal rhythm. (Here we meet with the coincidence of two features—a particular case which does not contradict the general order.) Therefore, the verse word is always an object of several articulatory categories at once, which complicates and deforms the articulation to an extreme degree. Thus, each coincidence may be recognized as an easy articulation, and each failure to coincide as a difficult articulation. (See B. Tomashevskii, op. cit.)

A complication of this sort is characteristic not only for the one articulating, but also for the one listening. (Consider Saran's persistent usage of the term *Stärkeabstufungen* in relation to the acoustic phenomena.)

The motor-forces characterization of rhythm coincides with the hierarchy of rhythmical elements. The major component of rhythm is meter. Factors of "instrumentation," of rhyme, etc., may be absent, but once the sign of rhythm is given, then along with this is given the sign of meter as a necessary condition of rhythm. Perhaps this is partially connected with the fact that meter deforms the sentence in the accentual respect, redistributing strength to a certain degree, and, via this, more than any other component, complicates amd pushes forward the motor-forces side of speech. (This is especially true in relationship to the Russian accentual system.) This corresponds to the evidence of the poets on the difficulty of metrical verse speech. Zhukovskii, preparing to write a "tale for young people," was worried that "the story, in spite of the difficulty of the meter, flows like simple, unconstrained speech" (Pletnev, vol. III, p. 123-4). Because of this, Zhukovskii weakened the perception of the meter in every way possible.

Thus, definite metrical systems apparently have a sharply individual motor-forces characteristic.

Here, perhaps, in the diverse coloring of diverse meters, it would be proper to search for an answer to the phenomenon that some metrical systems prove to be connected with a definite melody. B.M. Eikhenbaum calls this a fact of "reflected melodics" (*Melodika stikha*, p. 95-6). Apparently, one should search in the motor-forces characteristics of definite meters for their connection with a definite melody. I will introduce the curious evidence of a poet of the beginning of the nineteenth century:

> Some writers maintain that in similar shephards' arguments (this concerns the form of the idyll), not only the number of lines in the verses, but even the very measures of the above-mentioned should be quite identical in both singers. Having retained the first, I have allowed myself to deviate from the second, for I am convinced that if the measure of the song may serve (upon a reading) as some type of substitute for the voice or the melody, then the distinction of the above creates the possibility of ascribing to the song of one or the other characters distinct sounds. (*Idylls* of Vl. Panaev, St. Petersburg, 1820, p. 46).

"Instrumentation" as a factor of rhythm also conforms to the motor-forces characterization of verse. (See B.M. Eikhenbaum's *Anna Akhmatova*, 1923. B.V. Tomashevskii, op. cit.)

Viewing sounds of speech as a complex unity and equating them with music is a mistake which in recent times was maintained by the Symbolists. The very term "instrumentation" is therefore doomed to destruction. The concept of "instrumentation" is not new, but goes back to the 18th century. The theory of the 18th century was connected for the most part with the concept of "onomatopoeia" (Lomonosov, Derzhavin, Shishkov), but not the concept of "harmony" (Batiushkov).

It is curious that already in the end of the 18th century the acoustic theory of onomatopoeia was complicated by the recognition of the importance of the articulatory feature, which approaches the theory of a "phonetic metaphor." Consider S. Bobrov:

> Reading the original of this elevated and Parnassian harmony, I immediately feel the pure and free striving of vowels, especially where a storm at sea is depicted: the tearing of sails, the creak of parts of the ship, and the shipwreck itself; or, during a battle the aiming of the spear, or the arrows released from the hands of warriors. Reading in the famous Prince the golden words and sweet ringing of Vergil's hemistich—Vorat aequore vortex—or Horace's dancing feet— ter pede terra—I feel this pure and free striving of vowels, or of a short foot before a vowel, or one consonant, or a long foot. And this striving and secret harmony occurs, of course, because of the prudent selection of the sounds of letters, and naturally teaches the meaning of the mechanism of language. In a word, by the very articulation I actually sense how the storm roars, how the whirlpool twists and the ship is devoured, or how arrows released from strong hands buzz in the air, and so on." (*Khersonida*, 1801, p. 9).

155

Roman Jakobson's observation that only consonantal repetitions are significant in Russian poetry is interesting (*Nov. russk. poez.*, p. 48). If this is so, then this phenomenon is connected with the fact that in "sound repetitions" ("povtory"), the articulatory feature is pushed forward. The acoustic nature of vowels in general is richer than the acoustic nature of consonants, while the articulatory character of consonants in general is richer than that of vowels.†

Facts of equivalents, stated by us as being contradictory to the acoustic approach, yield an explanation in the presence of the statement on the motor-force nature of verse. Equivalents become feasible in the capacity of a particular, articulatory potential. Omissions of a text indicating meter are especially typical here. The possibility of the equivalent, which is the possibility of making an omission equal in value with a line, is based on the fact that we give to this omission (it is all the same whether this is actually done or only potentially done) a particular element of motion (outside of vocal material). Without this, the following lines would be presented as lines which do not directly follow after the last line of the text, rather than lines which are separated from it by equivalents of lines (and not by a pause!).††

The concept of the motor-force basis of rhythm may not concur with the data of empirical psychological investigations. Quantitative prevalence of the acoustic, visual or motor type does not solve the problem in the least. Types of perception are diverse, and they all have an equal right to existence. But even if, for example, the prevalence of the visual type were to be proven, this would not cancel at all the status of Less or of T. Meier, which may be described as the precise, constructive restriction of the visual type in relationship to poetry. These and other types are restricted by their very means; the movement of perception and the play of association are connected with the construction and are aimed in a definite direction.

* See the experiments of Landry, and the work of S.I. Bernshtein.
** See B.V. Tomashevskii, "Problema stikhotvornogo ritma," *Lit. Mysl'*, 23, II.
† I feel that such a formulation of the question, correct in general outline, is in need of more detail. The infinite articulatory distinction between plosives and sonants on one hand, and such vowels as "u" and "a" on the other are sufficient grounds to raise the question of articulatorily-complex and articulatorily-meagre sounds, rather than of vowels and consonants. In any case, the coincidence of sound repetitions ("povtory"), as systems of rhythmical factors, with the general motor-force basis of rhythm does not call forth any doubts whatsoever.
†† The motor-force nature of rhythm would even explain the important significance of the verse graphic. Besides the designation of the unity of the series and the group, the graphic has its own significance. The revolution of the Futurists in the area of the verse word (resp. of rhythm) was accompanied by a revolution in the area of the graphic. (There was an article about this by N. Burliuk.) Consider such phenomena as the graphics of Mallarme, etc. The fact of the matter is that violation of an habitual graphic causes phonetic and motor images to arise which stand between the graphic and meaning. (These are effaced in normal writing.) See Paul, *Prinzipien*, p. 381, 382.

39. It is interesting to note the feeling of the writer of the 18th century toward the phonetic composition of prose. Consider the writing of Khrapovskii from 1796 on Catherine: "The cadence in the prose of the latest plays was mentioned, and it was inquired of me what had happened" (*Diary of A.V. Khrapovskii*, ed. N. Barsukov, 1874. p. 20). Derzhavin also writes about cadence in prose, volume VII, p. 573.

40. *Moskvitianin*, 1812, vol. II, no. 3.
41. Ibid.
42. Consider *The Journal of the Goncourt Brothers*, published by *Severnyi*

vestnik, St. Petersburg, 1889, p. 19. In the words of Flaubert:

> Do you understand such nonsense: working in order not to encounter the unpleasant consonance of the vowels in a line, or the repetitions of a word on a page. What for?

At the same time, we might judge the role which "rhythmicalness" (not rhythm) plays in prose by the following:

> "Imagine," said Gautier, "the other day Flaubert said: 'Of course I still have ten pages to write, but I already have the endings of the phrases in my head.' So he thinks he hears the musical ending before writing the phrases, having already completed these endings. It is a funny method whether it is true or not. I think that the phrase principally needs to have an outer rhythm. For example, a very broad phrase in the beginning should not end too suddenly, unless this consists of a special effect. It is necessary to say, however, that Flaubertian rhythm often exists for him alone, and is not felt by the readers. The books are not made to be read aloud, but he shouts them to himself. The readers encounter in his phrases such loud effects, which to him seem like harmony, but which need to be shouted in order to receive the effect." p. 29.

Here Gautier (via Goncourt's narration) emphasizes perfectly the illegitimacy of placing the question with the center of gravity in the author's approach, and in his approach to the work (the "artistic will" of the author), wherein the basis of investigation is sought: "The books (i.e., novels) are not made to be read aloud," even if we do have Flaubert "shouting them."

43. Grammont, op. cit., p. 475.

44. Legras, *H. Heine, poète*, p. 165-6.

45. Tred'iakovskii, Smirdin edition, 1849, vol. I, p. 123-5 (*Russian Versification: Theories of Tred'iakovskii, Lomonosov, and Kantemir*, ed. and trans. by Rimvydas Silbajorts, Columbia U. Press, New York, 1968, p. 101-2).

46. Jean-Paul, *Vorschule d. Aesth.*, Hempel edition, II, p. 336.

47. "On the Sublime," the work of Dionysius Longinus, trans. by Iv. Martynov, 1826, p. 260.

48. Meumann, op. cit., p. 397.

49. A. Schlegel, *Berlin Lectures (Berliner Vorlesungen), III, p.* 208-209, Heilbronn, 1884.

50. Meumann, op. cit., p. 272.

51. The Russian language also reflects this dualism, with "znachenie" ("meaning") on one hand, and "smysl" ("sense") on the other. "To use a word in some meaning" refers to its usual meaning, while "to use a word in some sense" refers to an occasional situation.

52. Thus, the concept of the principal sign in semantics is analogous to the concept of the phoneme in phonetics.

53. *Ostaf'evskii arkhiv Kniazei Viazemskikh*, vol. I, 1899. p. 213.

54. Ibid. p. 219.

55. Therefore, the "law of binomiality" of Rozwadowski (*Zweigliedrigkeit*) is based on the fact that not only the "material" side of the word is significant, but the formal side as well. In any case, this does not abolish the general outlines of the scheme of principal and secondary signs. It only makes the question more profound, placing the principal and secondary signs in dependence on some alteration of either the material or formal part of the word.

56. Of course, this is also owing to the alteration of the vocal structure, which

colors everything it touches. Here I have deliberately isolated the question of the structure, focusing attention on the lexical coloring.

57. Also consider such groups as "zheleznaia doroga" ("railroad"), "belaia noch'" ("white night"), etc.

58. In the "restaurant" word usage, the use of the word "man" applied to a serf probably had an influence here. It also was used only with an effaced principal sign ("100 men" in the sense of "100 serfs"). Secondary signs were then joined to it, which quite displaced the principal sign: man—serf, servant ("his man"). Thus, before us in an alternation of meaning brought about by a concrete social fact.

59. "Irradiation." a term of M. Bréale. See his *Essai du Semantique*, p. 43-47.

60. H. Paul, "Uber die Aufgaben d. Wissenschaftl. Lexikologie," sec. 58. Sitzber., Der philos.-phil. Klasse d. Bayr. Ak. D. Wiss., 94.

61. H. Paul, *Prinzipien d. Sprachgeschicte*, p. 252.

62. Wölfflin, *B. Aufg. de. Thes. linguae latinae*, Sitzber., 94, p. 99.

63. L. Maikov, *Pushkin*. 1899, p. 300.

64. From this point of view, Shishkov's scene for children is interesting, written in a dialect which did not exist.

65. Consider especially the style of the popular intellectual letter from the middle of the 19th century: "poslanie tvoe poluchil" ("priial") ("I received your epistle"), "sei muzh" ("this husband"), and so on.

66. L. Maikov, op. cit., p. 311.

67. "An attribute such as an adjective, contained in the middle of a clause and coming *before* that which it defines, is never isolated: the only word which it is grammatically and logically connected with in such cases is its own proper definition, which stands after it. Consequently, the possibility of a correlative of the preceding stress is excluded." (Peshkovskii, *Russkii sintaksis v nauchnom osveshchenii*, Moskva, 1914, p. 283.)

68. To Polonskii, as cited by me, this was a recognized artistic device, completely comprehensible to the critics of his time. Thus, Strakhov wrote: "Whoever does not feel the special, original turn, the special manner of the following verses:

Uzhe nad el'nikom, iz za vershin koliuchikh
Siialo zoloto vechernikh oblakov,
Kogda ia rval veslom gustuiu set' plovuchikh
Bolotnykh trav i vodianykh tsvetov...

Already over the fir-grove, from behind the prickly tops
Shone the gold of evening clouds,
When I plucked with an oar a thick net of floating
Marsh grasses and water flowers...

will never understand it. It is not in his type of parts" (N. Strakhov, *Zametki o Pushkine i drugikh poetakh*, St. Petersburg, 1808, p. 160).

69. I deliberately cite a fragment of Maiakovskii where there is almost no action of *rhyme*.

70. "Just as there are wheels of gears which we are used to seeing adjoining one another, so that we do not present them as being separate, so in language there are words whose usages are connected so tightly, that they are not able to exist in our consciousness in an isolated state" (M. Bréale, *Essai du Semantique*, 1904, p. 172.)

71. Consider. A. Rosenstein, *Die psych. Bedingungen des Bedeutungswechsels der Worter*, 1pzg., 1884, p. 26.

72. Bréale writes concerning this that:

It is neither direct contiguity nor concrete proximity that is at the bottom of meaning. The inflection occurs through the general sense of a phrase. (op. cit., p. 207).

Wundt enlarges the term. He introduces in his work such examples as *universitas* (= formerly *universitas scholarum, universitas litterarum*), and *bonne* (= formerly *bonne domestique*), *Volkerps.*, II, p. 507), and thus he considers *"voisinage materiel"* as one of the causes of *"contagion."*

73. Longinis. op. cit., p. 167-173.

74. *Works and Correspondence of P.A. Pletnev (Sochineniia i perepiska P.A. Pletneva)*, vol. I, 1885, p. 24-25.

75. The series of *historical* mistakes of A.S. Shishkov do not diminish, but rather redouble the interest of many of his linguistic observations. The opponents who ridiculed Shishkov (Makarov, Dashkov, and others) up to now have not attempted to treat the valuable linguistic evidence given in the theory of "ranges" (*"krugov"*) and in the theory of the "root word" (*"korneslovii"*) precisely as semasiology.

76. A.S. Shishkov *Collected works and Translations (Sobranie sochinenii i perevodov)*, vol. XII, 1828, p. 127-29.

77. *Russian Antiquity (Russkaia starina)*, vol. XI, 1884, p. 198.

77a. *Works of I.V. Kireevskii (Sochineniia I.V. Kireevskii)*, vol. I, 1861, p. 15 Letter to A.I. Koselev.

78. *Conversations with Goethe*, op. cit., p. 285-86.

79. Rosenstein, op. cit., p. 70.

79a. W. Wundt, *Foundations of Psysiological Psychology (Osnovy fiziologicheskoi psikhologii)*, III, p. 16.

80. N. Polevoi, *Essays on Russian Literature (Ocherki russkoi literatury)*.

81. A.O. Smirnova, *Dnevn. (Journal)*, part II, p. 328.

82. Oxymoron is the combination of an attribute with some word defined according to its principal sign, where the principal signs of the words are contradictory: "bessmertnaia smert' " ("undying death") or "bessonnyi son" ("sleepless sleep"). Each oxymoron plays on the double semantics. The two fold connection occurs 1) according to the contrary principal sign being defined ("bes *son* nyi son") (*"sleep* less sleep"), and 2) according to the principal sign which is being defined and the principal sign of the epithet (*"bessonyi* son") (*"sleepless* sleep"). As soon as this connection, i.e., the recognition of the opposition of the principal signs, becomes habitual, it retreats into the background, and the connection only occurs between the principal sign of that which is defined and the principal sign of the epithet. This process of becoming colorless might be ascertained by attempting to substitute the resulting definition with another, so that the group meaning is not very altered. It might not violate this meaning too much to change "son naiavu" ("waking dream") into "volshebhyi son" ("magic dream") and so on. The habitual use of such an oxymoron might turn it into a group *with a single meaning for both members.* (This corresponds with the emergence of a single general principal sign at the expense of the signs of the individual members.) Such a transformation is easy to ascertain. One need only to attempt to substitute for a group a single word. On the way to becoming colorless the oxymoron "son na iavu" ("waking dream" literally means "dream in reality") is used in verse as a group. However, in the unification of this group with the preceding epithet "v elekricheskom" ("in an electric") into the phrase "V elektricheskom sne najavu" ("In an electric day dream") only "electric" and "dream" are coordinated. But it is in the word "sne" ("dream"), the first member of the group, that the redistribution of the group occurs, thereby creating the oxymoron. It comes out as:

V elektricheskom sne/naiavu
In an electric dream/while awake

83. It is interesting that before the recognition of this role of auxiliary words they were not connected by the principal sign. Prince Viazemskii wrote I.I. Dmitriev in 1835:

I am completely in agreement with you concerning the translation of Shevryev: In his language and verses incorrectness often appears, recalling Merzliakov who, in the words of Zhukovskii, *lived by begging from neighbors* when the genuine or proper word did not fall from his pen or would not fit into a line." (*Russkii arkhiv*, 1868, p. 642).

84. Words (and their substitutes) which have a "spatial" meaning I emphasize by spacing out the letter; words which have acquired it I have put in bold face.

85. Potebnia, *From Notes on Russian Grammar (Iz zapisok po russkoi grammatike)*, vol. III, Khar'kov, 1899, p. 35-6.

86. *Uhlands Werke*, hrsg. von L. Fränkel, I, p. 177.

87. On compound epithets by Lomonosov see A. Budilovich *Lomonosov as a Writer (Lomonosov kak pisatel')*, St. Petersburg, 1871. On compound epithets by Zhukovskii see A. Veselovskii, V.A. Zhukovskii, 1912, p. 453-4. The contrasts here between the tendency of the archaists and the Karamzinians are interesting to trace through the comparison of the opinion of Karamzin with the opinion of the archaists. Karamzin writes:

The authors or translators of our spiritual books have formed their language totally according to the Greek. They have placed prepositions everywhere; they have stretched and *combined many words,* and this chemical operation has changed the primitive purity of the Old Church Slavic." (Karamzin, *O russkoi grammatike frantsuza Modriu,* Smirdin edition, III, p. 604.)

In return Shishkov extracts the opinion of Voltaire that, "le plus beau de tous les langages doit etres celui qui a... le plus de mots composes" (In very beautiful language we must consider... most of all the compound words) (vol. II, p. 439). In an 1821 *Son of the Fatherland (Syn Otechestva)*, (No. 39, p. 273-4) Voeikov enumerates the compound epithets of Raich, reproaching him in imitation of Derzhavin. This list already resembles Tiutchev.

In an 1830 *Galateia* (No. 18, p. 89-90) see a sympathetic opinion concerning the stylistic methods of the archaists. S. Bobrov's use of them is especially strong.

88. On the phonetic principle of *composita* selection and the selection of compound epithets see L.P. Jakubinskii, in particular his article in the collection *Poetika*. I discuss the special semantic meaning of sound repetitions below.

89. Consider my article "The Question of Tiutchev" ("Vopros o Tiutcheve"), *Kniga i revoliuciia*, No. 3, 1923.

90. Consider what L.V. Shcherba says about "compactness of inversions," "Experiments in linguistic interpretation of verses" ("Opyty lingvisticheskogo tolkovaniia stikhotvorenii"), *Russkaia rech'*, collection I, 1923, p. 45-7.

91. Lomonosov, *Works (Sochinenii)*, Sukhomlinov edition, vol. III. p. 47.

92. Already, in the capacity of a biblicalism, the word is carried according to two series: "Runs at the mouth" (Mark 9, 18) meaning "to run at the mouth," to emit foam, *spumare*; and "running": "and immediately stopped her running blood" (Luke 8, 44).

93. It will be effaced because of the general condition of the metaphor which is guided, in the given case, by the "biblicalism": not only "the regiment runs" or the collective noun "the army runs," but also "Peter runs" will much more likely exclude the feature of their *collision* because of the absence of the correlation of the principal

signs. In spite of this, the metaphoricalness—the collision of the principal signs—has already disappeared. However, the unbound feature has remained. Thus, "Peter runs" will be "more generally" "less concrete" than "Peter goes." The colorlessness of the metaphor does not make it an equitable, homogeneous word, but rather a word with a more colored principal sign. Its proper principal sign is lost. The principal sign colliding with it has not entirely displaced it; it has not occupied its place completely.

94. *Literaturnaia gazeta*, 1830, p. 17.

95. See S. Lur'e "Observatinuculae Aristophanes" ("Brief observations on Aristophanes"), *Zhurnal Ministerstva nordnogo prosveshcheniia*. 1917.

96. It is interesting that in the 18th century the theory of onomatopoeia had already been replaced by the theory of articulatory expressiveness. (Consider S. Bobrov, in the preface to *Khersonida*.)

97. Consider S.D. Balukhatyi, "Nekot. ritm.—sintaks, kateg. russkoi rechi," Isv. Sam. G.U., no. 3, p. 5-7.

98. Paul, *Prinzipien*, s. 181; Wundt, *Vps.*, I, p. 623-624.

99. The semasiolization ("semasiologizaciia") of syllables may even have an influence on lexical selection. Thus, the purist A.I. Turgenev corrected Viazemskii's use of "posviativshis'" to "posviativ sebia," because "sh" should not be allowed in a word. Viazemskii wrote the following on this matter:

> Such ridiculous squeamishness! You are like that cure, who, in some novel of Pigault-Lebrun, excluded from his speech all swear syllables and said: 'Je suis tent,' instead of "content" and so on. In France, the word *pouvoir*, although even there is nasty, does not strike one as a curse word. (Ostaf'evskii Arkh., II, p, 261, 264).

100. Nyrop, *Das Leben der Wörter*, p. 192.

101. It is characteristic that in wishing to speak about progressive associations in rhyme, Viazemskii indicates the regressive associations with these lines. Without a doubt, the second rhymed member "Kheraskov" called forth the first member "laskov," and not vice versa.

102. S. Bobrov, *Tavrida*, 1798; 2nd ed. of *Khersonida*, 1804, p. 6.

103. Nyrop, op. cit., p. 125.

104. Such are the "nonverbal" rhymes of Shikhmatov. One should not forget, however, that each such prohibition limits the character and quantity of words which may rhyme. In turn, this leads to habitual associations which may then result in a reverse current and in the violation of the prohibition:

> ...Na melochakh my rifmu zamorili...
> Uzh i tak my goly:
> Otnyne v rifmu budu brat' glagoly.
>
> Pushkin, Domik v Kolomne

> ...On trifles we overworked rhyme...
> And even now we are naked:
> From now on I will take verbs for rhyme.
>
> Little House in Kolomna

105. Consider O. Hey, *Semasiologische Studien*, and Nyrop, p. 186.

106. Druzhinin, *Soch.*, 1867 edition, vol. 8, p. 38-39.

107. A. Schlegel, *Berl. Vorles.*, p. 168.

108. Quintilianus, VIII, 6, 4. Also See Potebnia's *Iz zap. po t. slov.*, p. 203.

109. A. Rosenstein, op. cit., p. 18.
110. Consider the opinion of Anatole France:

> What is an image? It is a comparison. And one may compare anything with anything else: the moon with cheese, or a broken heart with a cracked pot. Therefore, images supply an almost infinite amount of words and rhymes."

Conversations with Anatole France (Besedy Anat. France), sobr. P. Gzellem, 1923, p. 119.

111. Goethe, *Razgovory s Ekkermanom*, vol. I, p. 91 [*Conversations with Goethe*].

The Poetics of Verse Language
Brent L. Harvey

There are two distinct, but not incompatible, approaches to theoretical poetics. The first is concerned with the procedures of historical (re)discovery and (re)development, a kind of archeology of poetics. The better of these studies have their merit not in terms of their revivalist tendencies, but rather in their bringing forth material for comparative poetics, and opening the way for a deeper understanding and critical view of the international foundations of poetics. The second comtemplates moving beyond, or outside, the proposed theoretical framework and attempts to account for (either through modification or subsumption) the accepted theoretical observations with a more comprehensive analysis. There are a number of studies which purport doing the first of these, while the second—a genre to which Tynianov's work would lay claim—encompasses what we would think of as those pioneering works of modern poetics. What I propose to do here is to examine on a selective basis the underpinning of two of the theoretical issues related to Tynianov's poetics in *The Problem of Verse Language*, and to offer a few sources in which the interested reader can find material which directly or indirectly undertakes and reinforces the polemics of Tynianov's work. I have divided issues along the following lines: 1) Tynianov's methodological use of "equivalents," and 2) his ontological basis for verse-prose distinction.

Equivalents

Substitution, or the replacement of one item for another, became a fundamental test case in the development of modern linguistics, having its basis in, for example, Leibniz's "Law of the Indiscernibility of Identicals," or in effect a model for the "substitution of equivalents"—or more current to the time of Tynianov's work Husserl's development of categorial substitution in his investigation on "Pure Grammar"[1]—while, of course, "sameness of value" and "variable assignment" have been important for the semantics of mathematics as well as logic from their inceptions.

The semantic power of the equivalent is crucial for Tynianov's arguments, playing a central role in his overall picture of verse language. For his notion of "equivalents" Tynianov probably draws from Baudouin's use of the "equivalents of sound" as given, for example, in his 1877-78 lectures:

> *Phonetics, or, more precisely, the grammatical part of phonetics, investigates (analyzes) the equivalents of sound (sound units and their combinations) in terms of their specific properties, i.e., insofar as they play a role, for example, as soft and hard, simple and complex, consonantal and vocalic, etc., even though from a strictly physiological viewpoint, the phonetic equivalents of soft sounds may be hard, and vice versa, etc. The discrepancy between the physical nature of sounds and their role in the mechanism of language, as reflected in the feeling of native speakers (sic).[2] pp. 115-16 (Baudouin's italics).*

As we can see Baudouin gives precisely the notion of contextual determination that Tynianov employs, enabling Tynianov to generalize a wide range of "equivalents," e.g., the equivalents of meter, stanza, text, etc., all of which are based on the idea of a plane of meaning which is represented *in* the text. This level of meaning is generated through the assignment of variables which are introduced into the verse structure and are not meaningful independent of their verse context. We could think of this notion

163

linguistically (rhetorically) in terms of Jakobson's concept of *metonymy*[3], i.e., the contiguous transference of meaning from one item to another. An example which we might consider metonymic is cited by Tynianov when he refers to the "nose" in Gogol's story as an "equivalent of the hero"[4], that is the use of a part to represent the whole (synecdoche). However, in the case of the "equivalent of meter," used by Tynianov to argue against the acoustic approach to verse, it is not a partial metrical unit which is used to represent a larger unit, but rather the substitution of another element, namely dots, to represent the expected text. It is important that these dots do not *show* the meter, but rather *represent* it. Tynianov argues that because the dots can only be articulated as a pause, that therefore, on the acoustic account, they are relegated to the position of the other pauses in the verse, which are taken to be physical entities devoid of semantic content. Here, of course, we might recall Baudouin's distinction between the physical nature of sounds and their role in the language system. Although Baudouin's distinction is applicable here, Tynianov chooses to reject the idea that acoustic studies are able to account for the *role* of the pause in the verse system. However, it had already been shown with acoustics as early as 1918, in A. Snell's acoustic study of the pause, that the notion of a pause in verse has a psychological basis not an acoustical one.[5] As Snell points out the feeling of a pause is reported in those cases where its expectation is very high, e.g., at a caesura where the pause is acoustically signaled by the lengthening of the preceding syllable, not by the absence of sound. If expectations are allowed as determinants in acoustic studies, then we can talk about the semantic values of the pause in those cases where the reader's expectations are in conflict with the material presented, i.e., a pause where we would expect a rhyme or even a stanza.[6] In fact, verse ellipsis forces such an analysis. Even Mukarovsky, who leans heavily on Tynianov's work, makes the pause semantic in his position paper on the nature of poetic language:

> *An unusual use of pauses can also be thematically motivated, for instance by the excitement of the speaker. But even if there is not such a motivation, a pause is a carrier of meaning, for in intself it suffices to "signify" emotional excitement. A pause can even become the equivalent of a quite definite meaning if it is determined by its incorporation into the surrounding context... In verse there are rhythmic pauses provided by the rhythmic articulation as well as syntactic and semantic pauses... Pauses can even become temporarily the only carrier of the rhythmic and semantic context in verse. This happens when a line or even an entire stanza, filled out by pauses alone, occurs in the middle of a poem.[7] p. 31.*

It is not that Tynianov would question the semantic value of material ellipsis, actually he labors to establish this fact, but it is for him a question of both the genesis and the placing of that value. The reason Tynianov hedges on accepting the semantic value of the pause is not because of a failure to adhere to the kind of method suggested by the quotation from Baudoin, but rather is due to his unwillingness to treat the acoustic pause as an equivalent of rhythm, as compared his treatment of dots as the equivalent of text. Such a treatment, I suggest, would muddy an underlying distinction he wishes to preserve between meter and rhythm, on the one hand, and *representing* and *showing*, on the other. On Tynianov's account you can substitute for abstract categories, such as meter, stanza, or even word, and in doing so represent that category (in terms of its contextualized function), but you cannot substitute one material item for another and in doing so show the characteristics of the first item.[8]

For Tynianov, then, "equivalents" are a basic methodological strategy employed to keep the extra-verse elements in accord with his defining features of rhythm, and similarly to enable the introduction of extra-verse elements as factors of verse construction, thereby maintaining his overall view of the verse system. Saussure's views on identity in linguistics might help bring Tynianov's strategy into focus:

> ...*if a street is demolished, then rebuilt, we say that it is the same street even though in a material sense, perhaps nothing of the old street remains. Why can a street be completely rebuilt and still be the same? Because it does not constitute a purely material entity; it is based on certain conditions that are distinct from the materials that fit the conditions, e.g., its location with respect to other streets...*Whenever the same conditions are fulfilled, the same entities are obtained. *Still, the entities are not abstract since we cannot conceive of a street or train outside its material realization.*[9] pp. 108-109 (my italics).

This is the reasoning that stands behind the notion of the "equivalent" that we find in Tynianov, i.e., the very idea of evaluating the conditions of replacement rather than the material. As we have seen this is the reason that Tynianov does not use the concept of the "equivalent of rhythm," as rhythm is determined by a materially realized interaction of factors, while, on the other hand, meter is an abstract set of conditions.[10] Notice also that with the case of Gogol's "nose," the nose fulfills the conditions of a hero; however, it does not fulfill the material requirements—except, of course, in the ironic sense.

Returning to the issue of the acoustic approach to verse, we do find Tynianov pointing to its limitations. These are directly related to his strongest line of inquiry; namely, how does the meaning and lexicalization of a text interact with its verse structure, and vice versa?[11] This is a question which demands a rationalized model of rhythm and meaning, a model which Tynianov advances through a series of insights and examples.

Ontology

In putting forth his theory of verse, Tynianov does not use the word "ontology," nor would we expect someone giving a primarily functionalist view to be concerned with such matters.[12] However, in formulating his definition of rhythm, Tynianov not only discusses questions of use but also questions of facts or essences. The very idea of establishing a principle for the construction of verse, namely rhythm, is tantamount to an ontological claim. And even though the *role* of this constructive factor, or even the system underlying it (meter), is subject to change, the nature of the principle will remain intact as the defining feature of verse. This is to say that the function of rhythm itself is constructive, whereas the value (normative function) of rhythm (for example, iambic tetrameter) will be culturally determined along an historical dimension.

Rhythm, then, not only assumes the major role in Tynianov's ontology but also becomes a basis for generic distinctions. This by itself is not surprising; however, Tynianov attempts to define rhythm so as to give the necessary and sufficient conditions for verse, including free verse. In providing such an inclusive definition Tynianov characterizes rhythm with a set of material constraints rather than defining it in terms of a metric system. In this way he subsumes a deminition of the system of meter under rhythm itself. This does not mean that he loses the distinction, it means that the metrical impulse is not characterized by the factors of rhythm. The four factors for rhythm divide into two essential constraints: the first is a line constraint which operates over the verse series (i.e., the factors of unity and compactness); the second is an organizational constraint on the vocal material (i.e., the factors of dynamism and succession). This second set of factors broadens the concept of meter so that, for example, the metrical foot can be both accepted as a rhythmical unit as well as replaced by another unit—

say, for example, the word. With respect to the line, the broadening occurs by defining it outside both the notion of metrical quantity and syntactic boundaries. On this view the French *alexandrine* is as acceptable as a rhythmical constraint on the verse series as is the syntactical parallelism of *parallelismus membrorum*.

This definition of rhythm, as related to Tynianov's ontology, becomes clearest when Tynianov examines verse which displays what he says are its minimum conditions. This is when the presence of the fact of rhythm is minimal but yet is still constructive. Here we see Tynianov's rejection of the empiricist's approach to the prose-verse distinction. Tynianov claims that it is verse displaying the minimal conditions of rhythm that is the furthest from prose, thereby drawing a *precise* line between those texts in prose and those texts in verse.[13] There is, then, no continuum along which texts can be ranked with respect to their shared or overlapping features. For Tynianov the following diagramatic view of a verse-prose continuum does not hold,

free verse / rhythmic prose

verse   prose

whereas the view below of a systematic polarization does.

Verse   Prose
minimum maximum   minimum maximum
conditions conditions   conditions conditions

free verse   rhythmic prose

The generic line of demarcation is, therefore fully rationalized.

This has some interesting consequences for the philosophy of literature, as well as paralells in the analytic treatment of language and art. The issue that raises these parallels concerns the recognition of this line of demarcation or ontological gulf between verse and prose. The question is raised first by the empiricist who wishes to attack the second diagram in favor of the first. On this argument what Tynianov calls the constructive principle is seen as *in* the text; the argument then follows that prose printed as free verse blurs the generic distinction, as we don't want to have to say of this trick text that it now is verse through a mere form of mechanical reorganization; consequently, the whole endeavor of distinghishing verse from prose hinges on rhythmicalness which, as Tynianov argues, may be equally an element of prose construction. Thus a continuum emerges. A second argument is also given which accepts the idea that the constructive principle is not *in* the text, but argues that for this very reason calling a text verse is enough to make it so (*mutato nomine*), thereby reducing the ontological distinction to the willy-nilly ascription of the current purveyor. Because of a general dissatisfaction with this generic nominalism, this argument is turned to favor the notion that what really counts anyway is what the *writer* had in mind.[14] Neither of these views, with regard to the constructive principle and the text is never established by these arguments. This is where the first parallel with the analysis of language comes in. With language we have the ability to make statements which by the very fact of their structure carry an attendant commitment to the existence of our (the speaker's) presupposition of some state of affairs.[15] For example consider the following sentence:

Beth stopped eating animals.

The maker of this statement is assumed to presuppose, as will the hearer upon accepting this statement, that Beth did at a previous time eat animals. The attribution of this presupposition to the speaker will be made by way of the implicature associated with this sentence itself, eve if by some misuse of the language the speaker does not believe that Beth ever ate animals. In other words, the implicature associated with this sentence is attributed to the speaker regardless of the speaker's intentions or beliefs; it is in *fact* of the language. On the other hand, the use of this implicature may vary according to its contextualization. The implied condition (that Beth did at some time eat animals) can be *given* to be understood by the speaker—in that context where the hearer does not have previous knowledge of Beth's eating habits—and it can be *taken* to be understood by the speaker—in that case where the new information is only that she has stopped. This is related to the shared beliefs and knowledge of the speaker and hearer. The parallel for the verse text concerns the confusion about whether the constructive principle is a presupposition (the writer's belief) or an implicature (as a result of the text). For Tynianov the constructive principle is a *fact* of the text; therefore, it is an implicature which in its uptake ascribes to the writer the belief that the text is *in* verse. This is why the sign of rhythm, according to Tynianov, is sufficient to make it verse, just as the sign of the belief is sufficient to establish the presupposition. As with implicatures, it is not true that the principle of construction is *in* the text, but it is conventionally implied by it; and like conventional implicatures it is not cancellable.[16] Just as you cannot say, and hope to maintain a conventional use of the language, "Beth stopped eating animals, however I don't mean to say that she ever did," you cannot compose a limerick and say, "but I don't mean for that to be rhythmical."[17]

This still leaves the parallel between the contextualization of the presuppositional implicature and the verse implicature, that is, the relationship between the implicature and its uses. By "uses" I mean, in the narrow sense, whether the text is *given* or *taken* to be understood as in verse. The similarity here is a little less clear; however, as Tynianov suggests, there is a difference between a sonnet—where I would suggest it is taken to be understood that it is in verse—and free verse, or in fact any text which has merely the *sign* of rhythm—where it is given to be understood that it is in verse.[18] It seems that any new form of verse initially is given to be understood as verse through its graphic form, like the first uses of stress meters in English or *dol'niki* in Russian, or experiments with the constructive factor itself, like the visual instrumentation of concrete poetry.[19] It is only when the antecendent of a verse form can be applied that we can speak of shared knowledge between the reader and writer, and this is also the point at which the focus will move from the form *as* verse to the material in verse, what Tynianov refers to as the automatization of verse. Whether or not new forms of verse convey a *sense* of rhythm remains to a greater degree a culturally dependent question.

The last area I wish to examine concerns the relationship between the constructive principle of verse, on the one hand, and the use of facts about the construction of art as essential philosophical features for its analysis, on the other. In a recent paper, Arthur Danto discusses the philosophical questions that emerge from an analysis of the logical relations that hold between film and the other arts. His particular concern is with film and drama. Although, like Tynianov, he is not occupied with classificatory systems *per se*, he does however pursue what turn out to be interestingly similar problems related to generic considerations. Even his method carries a familiarity:

> Let us stand back, for a moment, from this proliferation of cases and ponder the methodology which generates them. I am not engaged in botanizing, in seeking for a new classification of the arts. Rather, I am seeking for what may be philosophically relevant in film as an art. And one method for isolating philosophical relevance is to look for principles which must be invoked if we are to distinguish between things which are otherwise exactly alike.[20] p. 6.

It is in this area that he gives a pertinent analogy for the verse-prose distinction. This analogy is provided through his consideration of the difference between a projected slide of the title page of *War and Peace*, and an (ill-advised) eight hour film of the same page. Given that we could imagine a situation in which the projected images were shown simultaneously on the same screen and with no detectable visual difference, the question arises: Is there still a basis for differentiation? His affirmative answer points to the fundamental factor of film, i.e., the fact that motion is relevant in the case of film where it is not for slides. The film shows the title page not moving where the slide shows only the title page. The parallel is obvious, film like verse has, by a fact of its construction, the force to alter the material it displays, even though the material itself shows none of the features of this principle. On Tynianov's way of looking at this, the material is deformed by the principle of construction; here the film of the title page of *War and Peace* is altered and therefore deformed by the possibility of its movement, or for that matter any movement, e.g., the camera's stampede, there remains a difference between showing things in motion and showing things moving as film does.

These examples are aimed at giving an account of the constructive principle and its relation to the philosophical basis of Tynianov's theory of verse. The notion of "implicature" was used to point up the conventional aspects of the relation between verse-rhythm and the language system. And the analogy with film was discussed to highlight the rational, philosophical foundation of Tynianov's theory.

Conclusion

The focus of these comments has been quite strict, dealing first with the question of method and second with the philosophical relevance of the constructive principle and its divisive power. For the most part this concentration leaves unexplored Tynianov's theory of verse meaning. And it is to this application of both his method and his theory that Tynianov devotes the second part of his study. Therefore, by way of a conclusion, I would like to turn briefly to this application. In his second part, Tynianov deals with how meaning is contextualized under the influence of the constructive factor of verse; for example, how particular semantic relations are foregrounded by their position in the verse series. This is a shift from the philosophical dimensions described above to the cognitive and aesthetic results of verse form, and this provides an application which opens the way for a systematic view of poetic analysis. Poetic analysis is tied directly to the impact of verse on the combined philological, historical, and structural theory of meaning which he proposes. This strategy for investigation furthers his cause for rationalizing the structure of verse by placing rhythm in direct collocation with meaning. Even though his venture into practical criticism is more exemplary that it is thoroughgoing, the groundwork is laid for the semantic study of verse. This is the area in which the departure from 19th century poetics is perhaps greatest, as Tynianov concentrates on the development of lexical semantics with respect to the literary text. Although his theory of lexical meaning is a composite of his contemporaries, e.g., Hermann Paul and Michel Breal, his attempt at showing compositionally how the word both contributes to and is determined by its place in the literary text is a breakthrough for literary theory. And the question of how words determine the meaning of a text from the point of view of either its production or its comprehension remains a fundamental task for our current research in theoretical poetics.

1. Edmund Husserl's impact on and contribution to early structuralist thinking has been little noted until recently (see E. Holenstein's "Jakobson and Husserl: A Contribution to the Genealogy of Structuralism," *Human Context*, 7 (1975), 61-83, and for his attempt to give a more detailed account see *Roman Jakobson's Approach to Language: Phenomenological Structuralism*, trans. Schelbert and Schelbert (Bloomington: Indiana University Press, 1976). This is due in part because his *Logical Investigations* published in full in 1913 was not translated into English until 1970, trans. Findlay (New York: Humanities Press). It is interesting to note that Husserl's principle of substitution is an early form of what became a mainstay of structural linguistics, namely immediate constituent analysis.

2. Baudouin de Courtenay and other members of the Kazan school of linguistics laid the foundations for East European structuralism, as did Saussure for European structuralism. For a brief history of this movement see E. Stankievich's introduction to his translations of Baudouin in *A Baudouin de Courtenay Anthology* (Bloomington: Indiana University Press, 1972) from which the quotation is cited.

3. R. Jakobson, "The Metaphoric and Metonymic Poles," *Fundamentals of Language*, ed. Jakobson and Halle (The Hague: Mouton, 1956), pp. 76-82. Also, for a brief mention of metonymy in literature, as well as other major tenets of what has come to be called Jakobsonian poetics, see his "Closing Statement: Linguistics and Poetics," *Style and Language*, ed. Sebeok (Cambridge, MA: MIT Press, 1960), pp. 350-377.

4. This is a notion distinct from the mere particular-universal distinction for which any realized hero is an instance of the category "hero."

5. A. Snell, *Pauses: A Study of Its Nature and Its Rhythmical Function in Verse, especially Blank Verse*, Contributions to Rhetorical Theory, VIII (Ann Arbor, 1918).

6. There is always a danger in reducing one phenomenon to another, here the shift from accoustical representation to psychological perception. The danger arises in attempting to give a complete account from a single viewpoint, for example, from only the physiological or psychological. Tynianov clearly wishes to avoid such reductions.

7. J. Mukarovsky, "On Poetic Language," *The Word and Verbal Art*, trans. Burbank and Steiner (New Haven: Yale University Press, 1977), pp. 1-64.

8. Based on this analysis of substitution, the "foot-adding theory" (*stoposlagatel'naia teoriia*) of rhythmic prose developed by Bely and Shengeli was doomed to fail, as free bisyllabic and trisyllabic substitutions for the metrical foot will fail to *show* the characteristics of meter. The theory is inadequate for other reasons as well, see V. Zhirmunskii's "On Rhythmic Prose," *To Honor Roman Jakobson* III (The Hague: Mouton, 1967), pp. 2376-2388.

9. F. de Saussure, *Courses in General Linguistics*, ed. Bally and Sechehaye, trans. Baskin (New York: McGraw-Hill, 1959).

10. Zhirmunskii in his *Introduction to Metrics*, ed. Stankiewicz and Vickery, trans. Brown (The Hague: Mouton, 1966), puts this distinction quite succinctly, "Rhythm exists as the *interaction* of two things: the natural characteristics of the verbal *material*, and the compositional *law* of alternation, which is incompletely realized, owing to the resistance of the verbal material." (his italics) p. 21. Tynianov's definition of rhythm does not deviate however from Zhirmunskii's, but in a manner that is not immediately relevant.

11. The concept of an interaction of factors is basic to Tynianov's approach to the literary text. There have been recent attempts to broaden his work as a general theory of texts, see I. Even-Zohar's "Polysystem Theory," *Poetics Today*, 1. 1-2 (1979). 287-310. Also, for a model of interactionist theory of verse structure, see B. Harvey and K. Kao, "Text Generative Modelling of Chinese Regulated Verse." *Poetics*, 8.5 (1979), 459-479.

12. However, I don't wish to suggest by this that functionalism is synonymous with relativism; as we will see with Tynianov, it is not.

13. In defense of this Tynianov likes to call our attention to the peculiarity of reversing such notions as the "novel in verse," used by Pushkin to describe *Evgenii Onegin*; it is difficult to consider this work as equally a "verse in novel form," which seems to designate something else.

14. Tynianov touches on these arguments when he discusses the effect of displaying verse as prose and prose as verse. He is quick to dismiss the problem of the same text given as both prose and verse when he rejects as inconsequential Lagras's suggestion to consider Heine's *Die Nordsee* as prose.

15. Here I follow the view given by M. Huntley ("Presupposition and Implicature," *Semantikos*, 1.2 (1976), 67-88) that there is a distinction to be made between presuppositions and implicatures (i.e., the implications of a sentence or utterance). I also use the notion of the difference between "giving something to be understood" and "taking something to be understood" as a way of characterizing the uses of presuppositional implicatures. To my knowledge, Huntley is the first to see the difference in this way. For the spadework on these issues I refer the reader to his paper.

16. H. Grice uses cancellability as a test case for the distinction between "conventional implicatures" which cannot be cancelled and "conversational implicatures.. which can be cancelled. Grice's 1967 William James Lectures, *Logic and Conversation*, which have circulated in mimeographed form (a portion now appears in print in *Syntax and Semantics* 3, ed. Cole and Morgan (New York: Academic Press, 1975) pp. 4-58), are of primary importance in the development of a theory of language use (pragmatics). For a view of the relationship of this work to literary studies, see T. van Dijk, "Pragmatics and Poetics," *Pragmatics of Language and Literature*, ed. T. van Dijk, (Amsterdam: North-Holland, 1976) pp. 23-57.

17. I don't use recitation here because readings can go a long way toward obscuring the sign of rhythm. Consider, for example, the various recitals of dramatic blank verse. Although, in the case of the limerick, the rhythm would be difficult to obscure.

18. J. Culler goes a step further than this by demonstrating that a piece of journalistic prose when written as free verse can be subjected with some measure of success to the scrutiny of poetic interpretation, thereby giving evidence for the conventionality of the practice of poetic interpretation as well. *Structuralist Poetics* (Ithaca: Cornell University Press, 1975) pp. 161-64.

19. It is interesting to note that in verse which has no graphic sign there is generally some type of poetic designator, for example, early Chinese poetry, which was printed for economic reasons without line boundaries (as well as not having syntactic markers), was marked generally with poetic descriptors, like *fu* (e.g., "*Fu* on a small garden") which signaled a descriptive verse which often contained prose insertions, or, in the Sung dynasty, *tz'u* where the title consisted in naming the full metrical (musical) pattern for the text.

20. Danto's paper "Moving Pictures," *Quarterly Review of Film Studies, Winter (1979)*, 1-23, is an abbreviated version of his Matchette Lectures on Philosophy delivered at the University of Wisconsin-Madison in the spring of 1978. Tynianov also discusses problems of representation with respect to film in his 1927 paper, "On the Principles of Cinema," reprinted in Russian in *Poetika, istoriia literatury, kino* (Moskva: Nauka, 1977) pp. 326-345.

ACKNOWLEDGEMENTS

Thanks are due the following people for their comments during this project: James Bailey, Deborah Harvey, Richard Jacobson, Roman Jakobson, Karl Kao, Leta Kelertas, Arthur Kunst, Fannie LeMoine and J. Thomas Shaw, and also Carl Proffer and Marysia Ostafin for their help. A special thanks to John Schillinger. Misunderstandings in the translation or errors in my comments remain, of course, my responsibility.